XHTML

MIKE McGRATH

In easy steps is an imprint of Computer Step
Southfield Road . Southam
Warwickshire CV47 0FB . United Kingdom
www.ineasysteps.com

Notice of Liability
Every effort has been made to ensure that this book contains
accurate and current information. However, Computer Step and the
author shall not be liable for any loss or damage suffered by readers
as a result of any information contained herein.

Trademarks
All trademarks are acknowledged as belonging to their respective
companies.

Printed and bound in the United Kingdom

ISBN 1-84078-125-4

Contents

1   Introducing XHTML   7

The evolution of XHTML	8
XHTML introduction	10
XHTML tools	12
Mobile device simulators	13
Beginning a XHTML document	14
XHTML root element	16
Document structure	17
XHTML authoring tips	18

2   Head information   19

Head section	20
Document title	21
Meta information	22
Cache control	24
Format schemes	25
Adding scripts	26
Linking stylesheets	28
Linking other resources	30
Setting a base address	32

3   Body content   33

Content in paragraphs	34
Content in divisions	35
Forcing line breaks	36
Headings	37
Character entities	38
Quotes and blockquotes	40
Emphasizing text	42
Preformatted text	43
Contact address	44
Displaying code in text	45
Advisory elements	46
Keyboard input	48

4 Adding style to content — 49

Styling selectors — 50
Styling with class — 52
Styling by identity — 54
Styling spans — 56
Stylesheet efficiency — 57
XHTML colors — 58

5 Making lists — 59

Ordered lists — 60
Unordered lists — 61
Disc bullets — 62
Circle bullets — 63
Square bullets — 64
Decimal bullets — 65
Image bullets — 66
Definition lists — 67
Positioning list items — 68
List style shorthand — 70

6 Building tables — 71

A simple table — 72
Adding a table caption — 74
Adding column headings — 75
Spanning rows — 76
Spanning columns — 77
Aligning content — 78
Header information — 80
Categorizing cell data — 82
Abbreviated content — 84

7 Hyperlinks and anchors — 85

Creating a hyperlink — 86
Following links — 87
Fragment anchors — 88
Images as links — 90
Setting the tab order — 92
Describing the target — 93
Defining target relationships — 94

8

Embedding objects — 95

Adding an image — 96
Objects and MIME types — 98
Embedded image object — 99
Embedded text — 100
Embedded Java applet — 102
Embedded multimedia — 104
QuickTime & Real media players — 106
Flash movie player — 108

9

Using frames — 109

The frameholder document — 110
Two-column frameset — 111
Two-row frameset — 112
Nested frameset — 113
Frame appearance & targets — 114
Alternative content — 116

10

Creating forms — 117

A simple form — 118
Text inputs — 120
Checkboxes — 122
Radio buttons — 124
Selection menus — 126
Text areas — 128
Using labels — 130
Reset buttons — 132

11

Borders and margins — 133

The content box — 134
Background & border color — 135
Border styles & width — 136
Border shorthand — 138
Adding padding — 139
Relative padding — 140
Padding shorthand — 141
Setting margins — 142
Margin shorthand — 143
Putting it together — 144

Displaying content   145

12

Block display	146
Inline display	147
Electing not to display content	148
Wrapping text around images	150
Hiding content	152
Disallow wrapping	154

Stylish text   155

13

Font families	156
Font size	157
Font style & weight	158
Font shorthand	160
Text & content alignment	161
Text decoration	162
Indenting text	163
Spacing text	164
Line height	165
Text capitalization	166

Controlling backgrounds   167

14

Background image	168
Repeating background image	170
Positioning background image	171
Fixing background image	172
Background shorthand	173
Page formats	174
Cursors	176

XHTML Mobile Profile   177

15

What is XHTML Mobile Profile ?	178
List attributes	179
Style support	180
Presentation elements	182
Grouping elements	184
What's next ?	186

Index   187

Introducing XHTML

Welcome to the world of eXtensible HyperText Markup Language (XHTML) – creating Internet content for both desktop and mobile web browsers. This initial chapter examines the evolution of XHTML and demonstrates how to create a simple XHTML web page.

Covers

The evolution of XHTML | 8

XHTML introduction | 10

XHTML tools | 12

Mobile device simulators | 13

Beginning a XHTML document | 14

XHTML root element | 16

Document structure | 17

XHTML authoring tips | 18

Chapter One

The evolution of XHTML

Historically, the desire to have text printed in specific formats meant that original manuscripts had to be 'marked up' with annotation to indicate to the book-printer how sections of text should be displayed. This annotation had to be concise and needed to be understood both by the printer and the text originator. A series of commonly recognized abbreviations therefore formed the basis of a markup 'language'.

A modern version of this concept was the HyperText Markup Language (HTML) that was created for the Internet to determine how sections of web page content should be displayed in a web browser. This language defined a standard range of markup elements which were understood both by the page author and the browser software. These markup elements, known as 'tags', advise a browser how the author would like to have the content displayed.

HTML was devised in the late 1980s by a British scientist named Tim Berners-Lee while he was working at the Particle Physics laboratory in Cern, Switzerland. The simplicity of HTML lead it to become popular in the early days of the Internet with text-based web browsers.

A major development with HTML came in 1993 when a college student named Marc Anderssen added an image tag so that HTML could display images in addition to text. This version of HTML was then included in the Mosaic web browser from the National Center for Supercomputing Applications (NCSA) and became very successful. Marc went on to establish the Netscape web browser.

http://w3c.org

By the mid 1990s various web browsers that were fighting for market share began to add proprietary tags to effectively create their own versions of HTML. The governing body of Internet standards, the World Wide Web Consortium (W3C), recognized the danger that HTML could become fragmented by these proprietary additions and acted to create a common standard to which all web browsers should adhere.

Today Tim Berners-Lee is a director of the W3C and the latest version of the W3C HTML standard is the HTML 4 recommendation that is in widespread use around the world.

But HTML is not without problems...

- HTML is not easily extended or customized

- HTML is inadequate for automated data exchange

- HTML does not integrate well with other markup languages

- HTML parsing is often ambiguous

Web browsers have developed to accommodate incorrect HTML markup in an effort to be seen as increasingly 'user-friendly' but this has increased the size of the browser applications alarmingly – it is estimated that over 50% of the code in modern desktop web browser applications is provided to interpret sloppy HTML code.

This inefficient situation was tolerable on traditional desktop browsers but when Internet accessibility also moved to smaller handheld devices, such as PDAs and cellphones, the luxury of bloated browser applications became unacceptable. Handheld devices have limitations for which HTML makes no allowance.

XML is a meta language used to describe data – whereas XHTML is an XML application that provides display formatting.

Recognizing the need for a better markup language to meet the needs of modern browsers and handheld devices the W3C developed eXtensible HyperText Markup Language (XHTML). This is a reformulation of HTML 4 as an application in the eXtensible Markup Language (XML) that was designed for data-handling. XHTML offers significant benefits over HTML:

- XHTML is easily extended by using XML to define new tags

- XHTML is perfectly adequate for automated data exchange because it can be integrated with other XML-based languages.

- XHTML does integrate well with other markup languages because it can be used alongside any other XML application, such as MathML, Synchronized Multimedia Integrated Layer (SMIL), or Scalable Vector Graphics (SVG). Additionally you can create and integrate your own XML-based language if required.

- XHTML parsing is not ambiguous because each XHTML document must be well-formed and optionally validated against its Document Type Definition (DTD). This enforces correct syntax so that browsers do not need additional code to provide acceptability for erroneously coded documents.

XHTML introduction

The W3C members represent all the industries with any significant interest in the global development of Internet technology so the XHTML standard was created to satisfy all their requirements.

The W3C HTML Working Group described the new language like this: "XHTML is the keystone in W3C's work to create standards that provide richer web pages on an ever-increasing range of browser platforms including cellphones, televisions, cars, wallet-sized wireless communicators, kiosks and desktops. XHTML is modular, making it easy to combine with markup tags for things like vector graphics, multimedia, math, electronic commerce, and more. Content providers will find it easier to produce content for a wide range of platforms, with better assurances as to how the content is rendered. The modular design reflects the realization that a one-size-fits-all approach will no longer work in a world where browsers vary enormously in their capabilities."

Tim Berners-Lee, originator of HTML, commented "XHTML connects the present web to the future web. It provides the bridge to page and site authors for entering the structured data XML world, while still being able to maintain operability with user agents that support HTML 4."

Crucially, this new language was also well-received commercially by cellphone manufacturers:

www.nokia.com

"With this technology we merge the best of the web and wireless worlds" said Pertti Lounamaa, vice president of Nokia Mobile Phones, "And equally important to us and to our customers, it is a technology with great benefits for consumers that is also completely open and supported by the world's standards bodies."

www.ericsson.com

"Ericsson is very happy to see XHTML1.0 made a W3C recommendation. We are now able to see a realistic and rapid path for the convergence of the mobile and fixed-network web. Mobile devices already use an XML-based markup language (WML), and convergence of WML towards XHTML, as well as use of data from the web on mobile devices, is tremendously simplified by the W3C formalization of the XHTML specification. We have been working hard in both the W3C and the WAP Forum to enable this, and while a lot of work is yet to be done, this is a big step forward."

The original standard for mobile devices was specified by the WAP Forum which created WAP 1.0 using the Wireless Markup Language (WML). The WAP 2.0 successor to this specification abandoned WML and embraced XHTML in its place.

www.openmobilealliance.org

The WAP Forum was consolidated into a new organization called the Open Mobile Alliance (OMA) in June 2002. The OMA's stated aim is to "grow the market for the entire industry by removing barriers to interoperability and supporting a seamless and easy-to-use mobile experience for end users".

The W3C's XHTML 1.0 specification provides three Document Type Definitions that can be used to create XHTML web pages:

- **Strict DTD** – the standard that should be used for all XHTML pages that only contain fully valid XHTML markup code

- **Transitional DTD** – the standard that can be used where a XHTML document also contains older HTML markup code that is not valid in the Strict DTD

- **Frameset DTD** – the standard that can be used where frames are used to display XHTML pages in a multi-document web page. Small mobile devices do not usually have this capability so it is best to avoid using frames to display XHTML web pages.

The small size of display screens fitted to mobile browsers makes the display of frames impossible. It is, therefore, a good idea to stop designing web pages that use frames.

Importantly, a special subset of the XHTML 1.0 specification is defined in the XHTML Basic 1.0 specification. This contains all the components of XHTML except those parts, such as frames, which are inappropriate for small-device browsers.

It is the XHTML Basic specification that has been adopted for the standard of WAP 2.0 and it is also this specification that is featured in most examples throughout this book. XHTML Basic allows a single web page to be displayed both in a traditional desktop browser and in a browser in a smaller device, such as a cellphone or PDA. Stylesheets are used to format the content in a manner appropriate to the type of browser in which the web page is being displayed.

The examples in this book demonstrate each aspect of XHTML Basic and illustrate how the listed code may appear as output in both traditional and small-device browsers.

XHTML tools

XHTML code can be written in any basic text editor, such as Windows' Notepad application, and does not require any special software. The new text file can be saved with a file extension of '.html' then the output can be viewed in a web browser, such as Microsoft Internet Explorer, Netscape or Opera.

www.macromedia.com

The web developers' favorite authoring tool is the Dreamweaver application from Macromedia and support for XHTML was introduced in the Dreamweaver MX version. The major benefit of using Dreamweaver is that it quickly allows content to be created simply by dragging components onto a 'design view' of the page. Dreamweaver simultaneously writes the appropriate XHTML elements into the 'code view' of the page.

Usefully the Dreamweaver 'Commands' menu offers an option to 'Clean Up XHTML' which attempts to correct any code that does not comply with the XHTML specifications. This should ensure that the document code is 'well-formed' – without syntax errors. It does not attempt to validate the document against its DTD.

To validate the XHTML code written in a finished document it is best to avoid proprietary validator applications as these may not accurately adhere to the W3C specifications.

The W3C have a free on-line Markup Validation Service that will quickly validate the code of any XHTML document. It's located on the Internet at **http://validator.w3.org/file-upload.html**.

The validator has a 'Browse' button that allows you to choose the file to be validated. Once this is selected a click on the 'Validate' button runs the validation check.

If the validation fails the reasons are listed with helpful advice as to how they may be corrected. When the file is valid XHTML, the W3C validator offers a verification image that can be displayed on that page. This can prove useful to web developers to assure their clients that the code supplied has been tested to the correct standards. In any event, it is good practice to validate each new XHTML document before it is posted on the Internet.

Mobile device simulators

There are free simulators available that conveniently allow the XHTML developer to see how XHTML pages will appear on small mobile devices.

www.forum.nokia.com

The Nokia Mobile Internet Toolkit is available from the Nokia developers' website at **www.forum.nokia.com,** after completing a simple registration procedure.

http://developer.openwave.com

The Openwave Software Development Kit (SDK) is available from the Openwave Developers Site at **http://developer.openwave.com.**

Both of these simulators recommend that, if possible, the XHTML pages are tested via a web server. All the examples in this book have been tested via an Apache web server on the local system using the default domain name of 'localhost'. An alternative method would be to upload the files to an ISP then view them in these browsers via the internet.

The full support for all features of XHTML does vary between these two simulators – as it does with actual devices.

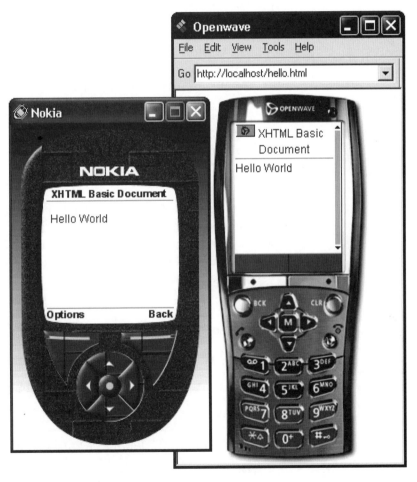

Both of these browsers are used in this book to illustrate the output of the listed code examples.

Beginning a XHTML document

As XHTML is an XML application each XHTML document should begin with an XML declaration that states the XML version. The XML declaration is contained within < and > angled brackets, like all other tags in XHTML, and looks like this:

```
<?xml version="1.0" ?>
```

The **?** character that appears immediately after the opening bracket and immediately before the closing bracket denotes that this is an XML declaration tag – the **?** character is not used in any other tag.

The term **xml** must appear immediately after the first **?** character without any spaces.

The **version** attribute of this tag is assigned the version number of **"1.0"** by the = operator. Notice that all values that are being assigned to attributes must be enclosed by quotes.

Optionally the XML declaration can specify a character set by assigning one of the recognized character set names to an **encoding** attribute, as seen in this example:

```
<?xml version="1.0" encoding="ISO-8859-1" ?>
```

The specified character set name in this example refers to the standard 'Latin-1' character set that is the default value normally used if the **encoding** attribute is omitted. Typically the encoding attribute could be used to specify a foreign language character set, such as those in this table:

Lots more character sets can be found on the website of the Internet Assigned Numbers Authority (IANA) at www.iana.org/ assignments/character-sets.

Name	Character Set
KOI8-R	Russian cyrillic characters
ASMO-449	Arabic farsi characters
greek7	Greek cyrillic characters
Shift_JIS	Japanese kanji characters
Big5	Chinese traditional characters

...cont'd

Each XHTML document must contain one of the following special **<!DOCTYPE>** tags after the XML declaration. These identify the name and location of the Document Type Definition (DTD) against which that document can be validated.

XHTML 1.0 Strict

```
<!DOCTYPE html PUBLIC
  "-//W3C//DTD XHTML 1.0 Strict//EN"
  "http://www.w3.org/TR/xhtml1/DTD/xhtml1-strict.dtd">
```

The character case in the <!DOCTYPE> tag should exactly match that of the listed code on this page.

XHTML 1.0 Transitional

```
<!DOCTYPE html PUBLIC
  "-//W3C//DTD XHTML 1.0 Transitional//EN"
  "http://www.w3.org/TR/xhtml1/DTD/
                          xhtml1-transitional.dtd">
```

XHTML 1.0 Frameset

```
<!DOCTYPE html PUBLIC
  "-//W3C//DTD XHTML 1.0 Frameset//EN"
  "http://www.w3.org/TR/xhtml1/DTD/xhtml1-frameset.dtd">
```

XHTML-Basic 1.0

```
<!DOCTYPE html PUBLIC
  "-//W3C//DTD XHTML Basic 1.0//EN"
   "http://www.w3.org/TR/xhtml-basic/xhtml-basic10.dtd">
```

Unless stated otherwise, the examples listed in this book use the XHTML Basic **<!DOCTYPE>** tag shown above.

In the code examples listed after this initial chapter the **XML** declaration and **<!DOCTYPE>** tag are omitted to save space – but please remember that they must start each XHTML document in order for that document to be validated.

XHTML root element

XHTML documents must adhere to the XML rule that each document must have one 'root' XHTML element that contains everything else. This root element is always the **<html>** element – everything is contained between **<html>** and **</html>** tags.

Optionally, the **<html>** tag may include an attribute called **xml:lang** that can specify the human language used in the document. The language is assigned as any one of the two-letter language codes specified in the ISO 639 standard. There are a large number of language codes but some of the more common ones are listed in the following table:

XHTML is a case-sensitive language – all tags have only lowercase characters.

Code	Language	Code	Language
en	English	**da**	Danish
fr	French	**sv**	Swedish
de	German	**no**	Norwegian
it	Italian	**ru**	Russian
es	Spanish	**zh**	Chinese
pt	Portugese	**ja**	Japanese
el	Greek	**ko**	Korean
tr	Turkish	**hi**	Hindi

To discover more language codes on the Internet, type ISO 639 into any search engine.

A typical **<html>** element, that defines its language to be English, would look like this:

```
<html xml:lang="en">
</html>
```

Each opening tag must have an associated closing tag to form a valid element in XHTML.

The <html> element may also, optionally, contain a **xmlns** attribute specifying the old standard namespace of **"http://www.w3.org/1999/xhtml"** – but this is not an absolute requirement as it will be supplied by the DTD if it is absent.

```
<html xmlns="http://www.w3.org/1999/xhtml">
</html>
```

Document structure

XHTML documents are separated into two parts between the **<html>** and **</html>** tags – a head section and a body section.

The head section is contained between **<head>** and **</head>** tags and provides information about the document. It must always state a title for the document between **<title>** and **</title>** tags.

The body section is contained between **<body>** and **</body>** tags and is the actual content that will be displayed by a browser. Text can be contained between **<p>** and **</p>** paragraph tags.

A valid XHTML document is listed in full below to illustrate the complete structure of a simple document:

hello.html

Save XHTML documents with a regular .html file extension – some browsers misinterpret the .xhtml file extension.

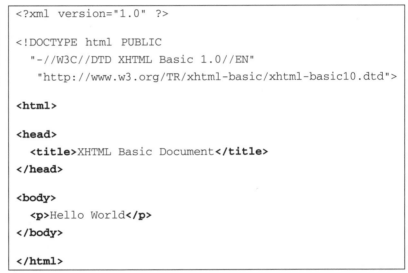

```
<?xml version="1.0" ?>

<!DOCTYPE html PUBLIC
  "-//W3C//DTD XHTML Basic 1.0//EN"
    "http://www.w3.org/TR/xhtml-basic/xhtml-basic10.dtd">

<html>

<head>
  <title>XHTML Basic Document</title>
</head>

<body>
  <p>Hello World</p>
</body>

</html>
```

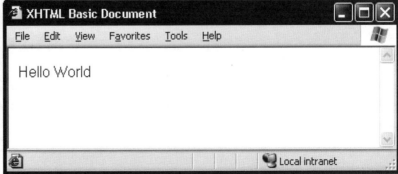

XHTML authoring tips

Comments can be added to XHTML code, across a single line or on multiple lines, between special **<!--** and **-->** comment tags. The browser completely ignores everything between these tags.

```
<!-- A single comment -->
```

```
<!-- A more lengthy comment
     that is spread across
     several lines of code -->
```

Lengthy comments may adversely affect the performance of small-device browsers so comments should be brief or omitted entirely.

Remember that all XHTML tag and attribute names must be in lowercase and that all attribute values must be enclosed by quotes.

Each XHTML opening tag must have a matching closing tag unless it is one of the single tags marked in the table on the inside front cover of this book. Those single 'empty' tags must always end with a forward slash character. For instance, **
** for a line break tag.

Elements must be correctly nested so that a closing tag does not overlap another element. This is a badly nested example:

```
<p>Here is a paragraph with emphasized<em> text</p></em>
```

A correctly nested version of this example would look like this:

```
<p>Here is a paragraph with emphasized<em>text</em></p>
```

The <em> and <input> elements are explained in more detail later in this book, together with their attributes.

Attributes must appear in full, complete with their assigned value, and cannot be minimized as they can in HTML. For instance, a checkbox input form component in HTML can specify that it should appear checked when the document is loaded by including the single attribute name 'checked' within the element, like this:

```
<input type="checkbox" checked>
```

In XHTML the attribute must also state an assigned value like this:

```
<input type="checkbox" checked="checked" />
```

Head information

This chapter explores the **head** section of a XHTML page and illustrates by example how it may be used. The samples show how to describe features of the XHTML document and how to add scripts and style sheets to the page.

Covers

Head section | 20

Document title | 21

Meta information | 22

Cache control | 24

Format schemes | 25

Adding scripts | 26

Linking stylesheets | 28

Linking other resources | 30

Setting a base address | 32

Chapter Two

Head section

The head section of a XHTML document follows the opening **<html>** tag and is used to contain information about that document.

This must always define a title for the document and also typically specifies keywords that can be used by search engines to describe the document. The document head section may additionally state the location of linked resources such as stylesheets and scripts.

In XHTML the entire head section must be contained within a pair of **<head> </head>** tags.

*The **xml:lang** attribute can optionally appear in almost any XHTML element to specify the language used by the content of that element.*

The **<head>** element may optionally include a **xml:lang** attribute to specify a language using the standard two-letter codes described on page 16 of this book. When this attribute is set the specified language will override any that may have been set with a **xml:lang** attribute in the parent **<html>** tag.

Additionally, the **<head>** element may optionally include a **profile** attribute which could be used in the future to specify the location of a meta data profile for that document. The format of meta data profiles, and how they might be used by a browser, is not yet finalized – so this attribute is intended for future development.

A head element featuring both optional attributes might appear like this in a XHTML document:

Remember that the required XML declaration and DTD declaration have been omitted from examples in this chapter to save space.

```
<html>

    <head xml:lang="en"
            profile="http://www.dublincore.org">

    <!-- head section information goes here -->

    </head>

</html>
```

More details on meta data are given later in this chapter.

The URL address assigned to the **profile** attribute above is, in fact, the home web page of the Dublin Core Metadata Initiative who are working on the development of metadata standards. It's interesting to visit their website from time to time to see how this project is progressing.

Document title

See page 38 for more on character entities.

Each XHTML document must specify a document title. There may be only one title and it should be contained within a pair of **\<title> \</title>** tags in the head section of the document. The title may comprise both regular text characters and entities for special characters such as ampersand, copyright mark and accented characters.

Typically, desktop browsers display the document title in the title bar at the top of the window. Smaller handheld devices usually display the document title in the header line at the top of the display. It is advisable to keep document titles short to avoid them being truncated to fit the limited area on smaller screens.

It is best to avoid using the document title as a replacement for text that should really appear in the body section of the document. For instance, on a page requesting the user to enter a password, text 'Enter password:' should be in the document body section – not just be the document's title.

The example below illustrates how a title may be displayed in both a desktop browser and a small-device browser:

```
<html>
<head>

   <title>XHTML Title Example</title>

</head>
</html>
```

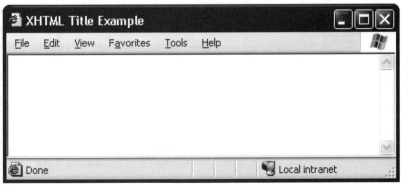

Meta information

Meta information is simply data that describes other data. In the context of a XHTML document meta data describes the actual document rather than the document's content.

Meta data is defined in the head section of the document using the XHTML **<meta>** tag. As this tag is only used to assign information to its attributes each meta element is an empty element – without an associated closing tag. In XHTML all empty elements must end with a forward slash character to denote they have no associated closing tag.

The **name** attribute of a **<meta>** tag is assigned a description of the type of data it contains while the actual information is assigned to the mandatory **content** attribute of the same tag.

Internet search engines typically look for a **<meta>** tag with a **name** value of **keywords** to establish which keywords should be associated with that document. The **content** value of that **<meta>** tag is a comma-separated list of appropriate keywords.

Each XHTML document head section may contain several **<meta>** tags stating various information about that document. The example below demonstrates some typical **<meta>** elements:

*The values assigned to the **name** attributes in this example are standard words that have special significance in defining metadata.*

```
<html>
<head>

   <title>XHTML Metadata Example</title>

   <meta name="author" content="Mike McGrath"/>
   <meta name="keywords" content="XHTML,easy,steps"/>
   <meta name="description" content="Guide to XHTML"/>
   <meta name="generator" content="Adobe GoLive"/>
   <meta name="revised" content="4th July, 2004"/>

</head>
</html>
```

The XHTML specification also provides a **<meta>** tag attribute called **http-equiv** that can be used with a **content** attribute to create 'meta-functions'. For instance, if the document contains time-sensitive information it may be desirable to specify an expiry date so that the browser is obliged to load the latest version of the page.

This can be achieved by assigning a value of **expires** to the **http-equiv** attribute and an expiry date to the **content** attribute.

*While desktop browsers do support meta-functions the **http-equiv** attribute is ignored by most small mobile browsers.*

Another common meta-function allows the page to be refreshed after a specified interval. This could be useful to update the page with fresh information, perhaps from a database or a CGI script. In this case the **http-equiv** attribute is assigned a value of **refresh** and the **content** attribute is assigned an integer value specifying the length of the interval in seconds.

Optionally the **content** attribute can also be assigned a new URL address so that the browser is redirected to this location when it refreshes after the specified interval. The address is assigned to a **url** query string following a semi-colon after the interval value.

The example below sets an expiry point for the document and specifies that the document should be refreshed after 30 seconds. When it refreshes, the browser is redirected to the address assigned to the **url** query string.

The expiry date must be specified in the exact format used here.

```
<html>
<head>
   <title>XHTML Meta Function Example</title>

   <meta name="expires"
         content="Sun, 4 Jul 2004 15:00:00 GMT"/>

   <meta name="refresh"
         content="30;http://domain/nextpage.html"/>

</head>
</html>
```

Please note that the **http-equiv** attribute is not supported by many mobile browsers due to issues concerning latency. It is included here for completeness but in practice it is best to avoid this attribute and to use server-side scripts for browser redirection.

Cache control

Both desktop and mobile browsers have a memory cache that stores each document the user visits so it may be quickly redisplayed without needing to request it again from the server.

The length of time that a device keeps a document in cache is called the 'time to live' (TTL). Typically the default TTL is 30 days – or until the memory is exhausted.

Browsers that support the **<meta>** element's **http-equiv** attribute can be instructed to ignore the cached document so they must always request the latest version from the server. This is achieved by assigning a value of **pragma** to the **http-equiv** attribute and a **no-cache** value to the content attribute, like this:

The success of this feature is unpredictable as many mobile browsers ignore the http-equiv attribute.

```
<html>
<head>
   <title>XHTML Cache Example</title>

   <meta http-equiv="pragma" content="no-cache"/>

</head>
</html>
```

This should really be regarded as a suggestion rather than an instruction because implementation depends very much upon the individual browser.

Similarly, a **<meta>** element can suggest that search engines should not list that document by assigning a value of **robots** to its **name** attribute and a value of **noindex** to its **content** attribute, like this example:

```
<html>
<head>
   <title>XHTML Robots Example</title>

   <meta name="robots" content="noindex"/>

</head>
</html>
```

Format schemes

The **<meta>** element has an optional attribute named **scheme** that can be useful to suggest a context to correctly interpret otherwise ambiguous data formats – such as those for date and time.

The following example uses the **scheme** attribute to determine the correct date format according to geographic location:

This example indicates that the date should be interpreted as April 5th – not May 4th.

```
<html>
<head>
   <title>XHTML Meta Scheme Example</title>

   <!-- Here scheme="EUR" implies DD-MM-YYYY format -->
   <meta scheme="EUR" name="date" content="05-04-2005"/>

   <!-- Here scheme="USA" implies MM-DD-YYYY format -->
   <meta scheme="USA" name="date" content="04-05-2005"/>

</head>
</html>
```

The **scheme** attribute generally provides helpful, non-critical, information to enhance the information in a XHTML document. A document about this book, for instance, could include its unique ISBN number in a **<meta>** tag and clarify what this number represents using the ISBN scheme, like this:

```
<html>
<head>
   <title>XHTML in easy steps</title>

  <meta scheme="ISBN" name="identifier"
        content="1-84078-125-4"/>

</head>
</html>
```

The **scheme** attribute is seldom used at present and is intended for future development, much like the **<head>** element's **profile** attribute that is described on page 20.

Adding scripts

The XHTML Basic specification does not support scripts because mobile devices are generally unable to process script code. Web pages that are intended for traditional desktop browsers can use the full XHTML DTD which supports **<script> </script>** tags that are used to contain script code.

See page 98 for more about MIME types.

The **<script>** element should include a **type** attribute that specifies the Multipurpose Internet Mail Extension (MIME) type of the scripting language being used. For instance, the MIME type for the JavaScript language is **text/javascript**.

Optionally, an alternative message can be stated between **<noscript> </noscript>** tags for those desktop browsers that cannot process the script. This should appear within **<p> </p>** paragraph tags in the document's body section, like this example:

script.html

```
<?xml version="1.0" encoding="iso-8859-1" ?>
<!DOCTYPE html PUBLIC "-//W3C//DTD XHTML 1.0 Strict//EN"
    "http://www.w3.org/TR/xhtml1/DTD/xhtml1-strict.dtd">

<html>
<head>
   <title>XHTML Script Example</title>

   <script type="text/javascript">
   alert("Hello from JavaScript");
   </script>

</head>
<body>
<noscript> <p>JavaScript is disabled!</p> </noscript>
</body>
</html>
```

This example uses the full XHTML DTD that supports <script> and <noscript> elements.

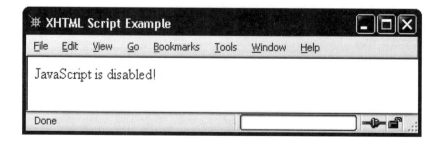

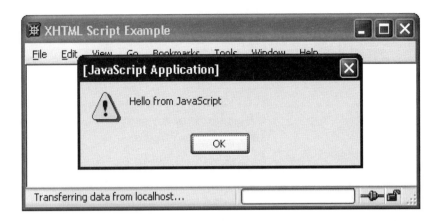

The output from the example will appear like one of the above screenshots depending on whether the JavaScript can be processed.

Script code can alternatively be placed in external files which are then made available to the XHTML document by adding a **src** attribute inside the **<script>** tag. This is then assigned the URL address of the script file so the browser can locate it. Notice that the DTD does not permit a single empty **<script>** tag so the element must still have a closing **</script>** tag even though there is no code directly between the two tags.

Please refer to 'JavaScript in easy steps' for more on interactive scripting.

The example on the previous page could be separated into two files by amending the **<script>** element to look like this:

```
<script type="text/javascript" src="myscript.js">
</script>
```

This states the location of the script file as a relative address – in this case the file is named **myscript.js** and it resides in the same directory as the XHTML document. Its location could alternatively have been stated as an absolute address giving a full URL such as **http://www/dir/myscript.js**. The script file is simply a text file containing just the actual script code without any tags, like this:

```
alert("Hello from JavaScript");
```

myscript.js

Linking stylesheets

External resource documents can be made available to a XHTML document by adding one or more **<link>** elements in the document's head section. This is always a single empty element so each **<link>** tag must end with a forward slash.

Each **<link>** tag must include a **href** attribute that is assigned the URL address of the external resource document so the browser knows where to find it.

See page 98 for more about MIME types.

Most frequently a **<link>** element is used to add a stylesheet that defines how aspects of the XHTML document should be displayed by the browser. The location of the stylesheet file is assigned to the **<link>** tag's **href** attribute and the MIME type of the stylesheet language is assigned to its **type** attribute. The stylesheets featured throughout this book use the Cascading Style Sheet language that has a MIME type of **text/css**.

*Other keywords that can be assigned to the **rel** attribute appear in the table on page 30.*

Each **<link>** tag should also have a **rel** attribute to specify the relationship of the resource document to the XHTML document from a range of keywords, such as **stylesheet**.

But the real magic of the **<link>** element lies in its ability to specify the type of device to which a stylesheet should apply according to the value assigned to its **media** attribute. Assigning a value of **screen** allows the stylesheet to be applied to traditional desktop browsers with large display areas. Assigning a value of **handheld** allows the stylesheet to be applied to small-device browsers with limited display areas.

A single XHTML page can be displayed both on **screen media** and smaller **handheld media.** Adding a **<link>** element for each type of browser allows the page content to be displayed in two different ways, in a manner appropriate to each type of browser, according to the rules of the relevant stylesheet.

To demonstrate this ability in action the XHTML document listed on the opposite page links two stylesheets that display the simple content in different ways according to the type of browser. The mobile **handheld** browser displays white, centered, bold text on black background. The desktop **screen** browser, on the other hand, displays black, un-centered italic text on a silver background.

...cont'd

stylesheet.html

These body
section tags are
described in the
next chapter and
stylesheet rules
are demonstrated in detail later
in this book.

```
<?xml version="1.0" encoding="ISO-8859-1" ?>
<!DOCTYPE html PUBLIC "-//W3C//DTD XHTML Basic 1.0//EN"
"http://www.w3.org/TR/xhtml-basic/xhtml-basic10.dtd">

<html>
<head>
  <title>XHTML Stylesheet</title>

  <link rel="stylesheet" href="handheld.css"
        media="handheld" type="text/css"/>

  <link rel="stylesheet" href="screen.css"
        media="screen" type="text/css"/>

</head>
<body>
<p>1st<br/>XHTML<br/>Stylesheet</p>
</body>
</html>
```

handheld.css

```
p { text-align:center; color:white;
    background-color:black; font-weight:bold }
```

screen.css

```
p { background-color:silver; font-style:italic }
```

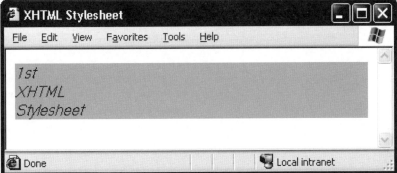

Linking other resources

A **<link>** element can be used to describe the relationship of another resource document to a XHTML document by assigning one of the keywords listed in the table below to its **rel** attribute:

*The **<link>** tag may also include a **rev** attribute to describe the relationship of a linked document to the XHTML document, using one of these listed keywords.*

Stylesheet	Alternate	Start	Next	Prev
Contents	Index	Glossary	Copyright	Chapter
Section	Subsection	Appendix	Help	Bookmark

When the relationship of the linked document is defined as **next** some mobile handheld browsers may download the linked document into cache. This enables it to be displayed without delay when the user wants to navigate to the next page.

The head section of an XHTML document may include several **<link>** elements describing a variety of linked resources. These may be used by search engines to determine the relationship between the documents.

The language used by a linked document can be specified by adding a **hreflang** attribute to the **<link>** tag. This can be assigned one of the standard two-letter abbreviations described on page 16. Additionally the character set used by a linked document can be specified by adding a **charset** attribute that can be assigned one of the standard character set names described on page 14.

An index page of a group of documents can be indicated by assigning a value of **start** to the **rel** attribute, like this:

```
<html>
<head>
<title>Reference manual — Page 5</title>

<link rel="start" title="The first page of the manual"
      type="text/html"
      href="http://domain/manual/start.html"/>

</head>
</html>
```

Search engines can be informed where to locate the printable version of an online manual by assigning a **print** value to a **<link>** element's **media** attribute:

```
<html>
<head>
<title>Reference manual</title>

<link media="print" title="The manual in postscript"
type="application/postscript"  rel="alternate"
href="http://someplace.com/manual/postscript.ps"/>

</head>
</html>
```

For web pages that have versions in other languages it is useful to indicate to search engines where the foreign language versions of the page are located:

```
<html>
<head>
<title>The manual in English</title>

<link title="The manual in Dutch" type="text/html"
      rel="alternate" hreflang="nl"
      href="http://domain/manual/dutch.html"/>

<link title="The manual in Portuguese" type="text/html"
      rel="alternate" hreflang="pt"
      href="http://domain/manual/portuguese.html"/>

<link title="The manual in Arabic" type="text/html"
      rel="alternate" charset="ASMO-449" hreflang="ar"
      href="http://domain/manual/arabic.html"/>

<link title="La documentation en Fran&ccedil;ais"
      type="text/html" rel="alternate" lang="fr"
      hreflang="fr"
      href="http://domain/manual/french.html"/>

</head>
</html>
```

*The entity **ç** creates a letter 'ç' – a 'c' with a cedilla. See page 38 for more on character entities.*

Setting a base address

The XHTML **\<base\>** element can be included in a document's head section to specify a default web location to which relative URL addresses in the document will be resolved.

For instance, if the **href** attribute of the **\<base\>** element is assigned the location **http://domain/dir/** any subsequent relative addresses in that document will be sought in that **dir** directory.

Note that when a **\<base\>** element is included in the head section it must appear before any element that refers to an external source.

The double-dot operator can be useful to refer to directories adjacent to the specified base location, as seen in this example:

Relative addresses start from the current directory by default.

```
<html>
<head>
   <title>CarParts Company</title>

   <base href="http://www.carparts.com/products" />

</head>

<body>

<p>See our <a href="../images/wheels.gif">wheels</a></p>

</body>
</html>
```

See chapter 7 for more on hyperlinks.

In this case the XHTML document is situated in the **products** directory that is specified as the base directory in the **\<base\>** element. This document's body contains a hyperlink to an assigned relative address situated in the **images** directory that is adjacent to the **products** directory of the same domain.

In this case the relative address is resolved to the full URL address of **http://www.carparts.com/images/wheels.gif**.

When a XHTML document contains a number of URL references to a single external directory it is useful to set that directory as the document's base directory. This allows each URL address reference to be stated as a relative address rather than its full absolute URL address.

Body content

This chapter demonstrates how to incorporate text content into the body section of a XHTML document. All the layout elements available in XHTML are described and examples of each one illustrate how they control the displayed text.

Covers

Content in paragraphs | 34

Content in divisions | 35

Forcing line breaks | 36

Headings | 37

Character entities | 38

Quotes and blockquotes | 40

Emphasizing text | 42

Preformatted text | 43

Contact address | 44

Displaying code in text | 45

Advisory elements | 46

Keyboard input | 48

Chapter Three

Content in paragraphs

Most text content in a XHTML document must be within a block type element. This may be either a **<p> </p>** paragraph element or a **<div> </div>** division element.

Separating text into sentences and paragraphs enables it to be more easily understood. Browsers will typically separate paragraphs by an empty line.

The example below displays two paragraphs illustrating how they are separated by each browser:

para.html

The **<body>** tag has no significant attributes in XHTML Basic..

```
<html>
<head>
    <title>XHTML Paragraphs</title>
</head>
<body>

  <p>
    Within its busy city life, Heraklion has many
    interesting features.
  </p>
  <p>
    One is the Venetian harbour - a good place to begin
    a city tour.
  </p>

</body>
</html>
```

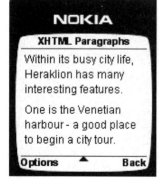

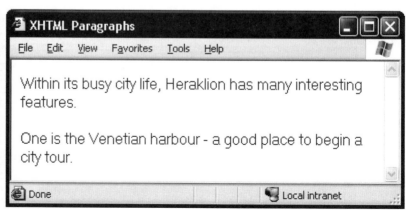

Content in divisions

The XHTML **<div>** element defines a section in a document that is typically separated from other content by a line break.

Unlike the **<p>** element a **<div>** element has no specific connotation attached to it. The author can apply whatever meaning is desired by applying stylesheet rules to the **<div>** element.

For instance, multiple **<p>** paragraph elements can be 'wrapped' inside a single **<div>** element so that stylesheet rules applied to that **<div>** element will cascade down to each of the paragraphs.

This simple example contains two **<div>** elements to demonstrate how each browser displays their contents:

div.html

```
<html>
<head>
   <title>XHTML Divisions</title>
</head>
<body>

   <div>
     Music is definitely the pulse beat of Crete.
   </div>
   <div>
     You'll hear it coming from radios, tavernas or
     people singing in the street.
   </div>

</body>
</html>
```

Forcing line breaks

When the body content is displayed text will, by default, wrap automatically to the next line after meeting the right-hand edge of the display area. The browser will normally seek back in the text to discover the last space at which to break the line. This ensures that the text wraps intelligently so that the last whole word is not split.

A line break in the text can be forced with the XHTML **
** tag. This is always a single empty element so it must end with a forward slash character.

A **
** break tag can be inserted as often as required and at any point in the text to force one or more line breaks.

Here the **
** break element causes two manual line breaks to the text content:

break.html

Although the Nokia browser shown below automatically wraps text some devices may provide a horizontal scroll facility instead.

```
<html>
<head>
   <title>XHTML Line Breaks</title>
</head>
<body>
  <p>
    The top attraction in Heraklion is<br/>
    the Venetian castle,<br/>
    still known by its Turkish name "Koules".
  </p>
</body>
</html>
```

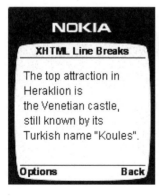

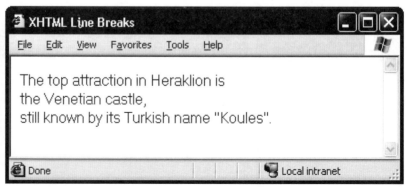

Headings

Headings in XHTML documents are used to define sections of text in the same way as the heading on this page. There are six sets of heading tags available in XHTML that range from **\<h1\> \</h1\>** as the most important, to **\<h6\> \</h6\>** as the least important.

Browsers will generally display headings in increasingly larger size to emphasize their importance. In addition, the browser could use the document headings to compile a list of topics that appear in that document.

The example below displays a range of different headings:

heading.html

Headings do not need to be contained within \<p\> or \<div\> elements like other content.

```
<html>
<head>
   <title>XHTML Headings</title>
</head>
<body>

   <h1>H1 Heading</h1>
   <h2>H2 Heading</h2>
   <h3>H3 Heading</h3>
   <h4>H4 Heading</h4>

</body>
</html>
```

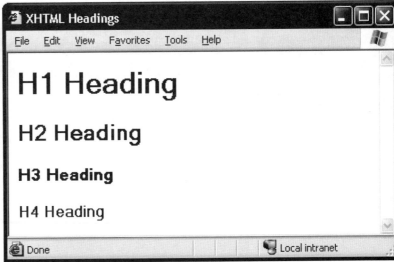

Character entities

Character entities provide a means to incorporate in a document those characters that are meaningful in XHTML itself. These are necessary otherwise a **<** character within the text content would be regarded by the browser as the start of a XHTML tag.

Entity references always begin with a **&** and end with a semicolon.

There are many character entities available in XHTML including those listed on the opposite page and the entire Greek alphabet.

Some of the most common entities are featured in this example:

entity.html

```
<html>
<head>
   <title>XHTML Entities</title>
  </head>
  <body>
<p>
      Spaces      Here<br/>
      Ampersand &amp; Quote &quot;<br/>
      Less Than &lt;<br/>Greater Than &gt;<br/>
      Copyright &copy;<br/>
      Registered &reg;<br/>Trademark &trade;
</p>
</body>
</html>
```

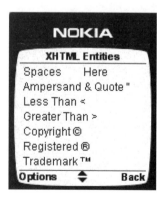

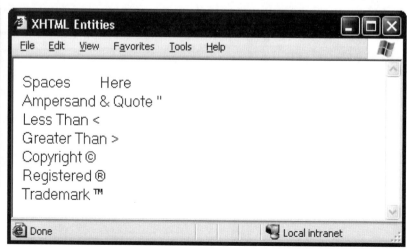

These named entities may alternatively be referenced by their numerical values. These start with hexadecimal   (or decimal) for   up to hexadecimal ÿ (or decimal ÿ) for ÿ.

To discover even more entities on the Internet type ISO-8859-1 entities into a search engine.

		¸	&cedil;	Đ	&ETH;	è	&egrave;
¡	&iexcl;	¹	&sup1;	Ñ	&Ntilde;	é	&eacute;
¢	&cent;	º	&ordm;	Ò	&Ograve;	ê	&ecirc;
£	&pound;	»	&raquo;	Ó	&Oacute;	ë	&euml;
¤	&curren;	¼	&frac14;	Ô	&Ocirc;	ì	&igrave;
¥	&yen;	½	&frac12;	Õ	&Otilde;	í	&iacute;
¦	&brvbar;	¾	&frac34;	Ö	&Ouml;	î	&icirc;
§	&sect;	¿	&iquest;	×	&times;	ï	&iuml;
¨	&uml;	À	&Agrave;	Ø	&Oslash;	ð	&eth;
©	&copy;	Á	&Aacute;	Ù	&Ugrave;	ñ	&ntilde;
ª	&ordf;	Â	&Acirc;	Ú	&Uacute;	ò	&ograve;
«	&laquo;	Ã	&Atilde;	Û	&Ucirc;	ó	&oacute;
¬	&not;	Ä	&Auml;	Ü	&Uuml;	ô	&ocirc;
-	&shy;	Å	&Aring;	Ý	&Yacute;	õ	&otilde;
®	&reg;	Æ	&AElig;	Þ	&THORN;	ö	&ouml;
¯	&macr;	Ç	&Ccedil;	ß	&szlig;	÷	&divide;
°	&deg;	È	&Egrave;	à	&agrave;	ø	&oslash;
±	&plusmn;	É	&Eacute;	á	&aacute;	ù	&ugrave;
²	&sup2;	Ê	&Ecirc;	â	&acirc;	ú	&uacute;
³	&sup3;	Ë	&Euml;	ã	&atilde;	û	&ucirc;
´	&acute;	Ì	&Igrave;	ä	&auml;	ü	&uuml;
µ	&micro;	Í	&Iacute;	å	&aring;	ý	&yacute;
¶	&para;	Î	&Icirc;	æ	&aelig;	þ	&thorn;
·	&middot;	Ï	&Iuml;	ç	&ccedil;	ÿ	&yuml;

Quotes and blockquotes

Within text content a quotation mark character " , or a quote entity **"**, is typically displayed by the browser as a double quote.

Alternatively, quotation text may be contained between XHTML **<q> </q>** quote tags. Typically these will surround the text with double quotes when displayed in a browser.

The added advantage of using a **<q>** element to display quotation text is provided by its **cite** attribute. This can be assigned the URL address of the document from which the quotation is taken.

This example demonstrates how a **<q>** element appears in a web page and assigns the address of the quotation's source document to its **cite** attribute:

quote.html

```
<html>
<head>
   <title>XHTML Quotes</title>
</head>
<body>
<p> Alexander spoke solemnly...

   <q cite="http://domain/plutarch.html">
   If I were not Alexander, I would be Diogenes.</q>

   - according to Plutarch.</p>
</body>
</html>
```

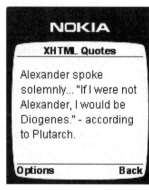

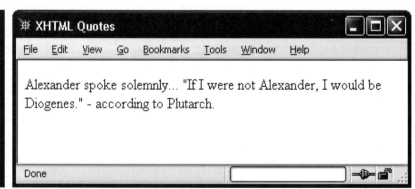

While the **<q>** element is suitable for very short quotations longer ones that can span several lines are better served by the XHTML **<blockquote>** element.

Anything between **<blockquote>** and **</blockquote>** tags is typically displayed on indented lines that set the quotation apart from regular text. Like the **<q>** element, the **<blockquote>** element may also contain a **cite** attribute to specify the location of the document from which the quotation has been taken.

The example below illustrates how the **<blockquote>** element displays a quotation in desktop and small-device browsers:

blockquote.html

Remember that, unlike the <q> quote element, a <blockquote> element requires an inner <p> paragraph element.

```
<html>
<head>
   <title>XHTML Blockquotes</title>
</head>
<body>
<h3>Edward Moore 1712-1757</h3>

<blockquote  cite="http://domain/gamester.html">
<p>I am rich beyond the dreams of avarice.</p>
</blockquote>

<p>- from <q>The Gamester</q></p>
</body>
</html>
```

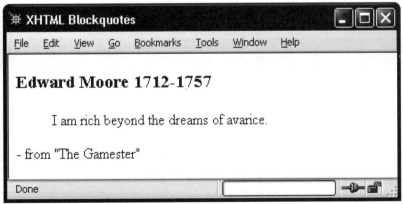

Emphasizing text

Text content can be emphasized in the browser by using **\<em\> \</em\>** tags or **\<strong\> \</strong\>** tags. All text between these tags will be displayed in an emphasized manner that is determined by the browser.

Typically the text in an **\<em\>** element is displayed in an italicized style and text in a **\<strong\>** element is displayed in bold font.

It should not be assumed that all browsers will choose this method as some browsers may use other techniques. For instance, a different font colour, an underline or a reverse background.

This example illustrates how each type of text emphasis appears:

emphasis.html

```
<html>
<head>
   <title>XHTML Emphasis</title>
</head>
<body>
<p>Regular text can be

   <em>emphasized</em>

   <br/>...or...<br/>Regular text can be

   <strong>strong</strong>

</p>
</body>
</html>
```

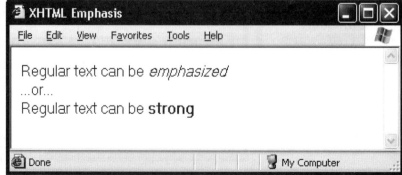

Preformatted text

The XHTML **<pre> </pre>** tags are useful to retain the format characteristics of preformatted text within a document. Any text between these tags will be displayed to include the original spaces, tabs and line breaks that are collectively known as 'whitespace'.

In the example below the preformatted text is displayed in a fixed width font and all the tabs and line breaks are preserved for the contents of the **<pre>** element:

preformat.html

*Notice the use of a character entity to produce the **á** at the end of each town name.*

```
<html>
<head>
   <title>XHTML Preformatted</title>
</head>
<body>
<div>On Greek signposts:

<pre>Chani&aacute;
    Xani&aacute;
        Hani&aacute;
            Khani&aacute;</pre>

...are all the same town!</div>
</body>
</html>
```

Contact address

The XHTML **<address>** **</address>** tags are useful to provide contact information for a document. These are often found at the beginning or end of a document to supply a link to a page giving more information about the author of that document.

The **<address>** element is also useful to provide information regarding the authorship of a particular form within a document.

In the example below the **<address>** element incorporates a hyperlink to another page about the document's author:

address.html

```
<html>
<head>
   <title>XHTML Contact Address</title>
</head>
<body>
<h3>Fun with XHTML</h3>

   <address>Author:
     <a href="mikem.html">Mike McGrath</a>
     <br/>Comments welcome.
   </address>

<p>The latest XHTML specification is great.</p>
</body>
</html>
```

In this case both browsers choose to display the address information in italics. For more on hyperlinks see chapter 7.

Displaying code in text

The XHTML specification provides three elements to describe pieces of computer programming code in a web page.

The **<code> </code>** tags are used to denote that the text contained between these tags is indeed programming code. References in the general document text to instances of a variable in the programming code may use the **<var> </var>** tags to denote a program variable and any samples of output from a program can be described between **<samp> </samp>** tags.

In the example below these tags are used to describe a simple JavaScript program in the general document text:

code.html

*The **<var>** element only denotes that the text is describing a variable – it does not declare a variable for use in XHTML.*

```
<html>
<head>
    <title>XHTML Program Code</title>
</head>
<body>
<p>In this JavaScript:<br/><br/>

    <code>var x="Hello";<br/>document.write(x);</code>
    <br/><br/>The variable <var>x</var>
    appears on the page as <samp>Hello</samp>

</p>
</body>
</html>
```

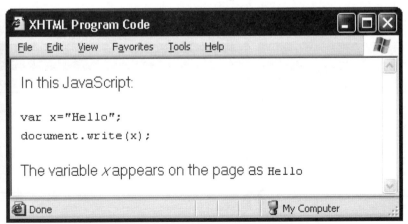

Advisory elements

The **<abbr> </abbr>** tags are useful to denote abbreviations and the **<acronym> </acronym>** tags denote acronyms. These could be used, for instance, to exclude their content from a spell checker. Additionally a style sheet could apply a particular style to all the abbreviations and acronyms that are denoted by these tags.

Optionally, both of these elements may contain an attribute named **title** that can specify the expanded version represented by the abbreviation or acronym.

Both **<abbr>** and **<acronym>** elements in this example include a **title** attribute explaining the abbreviation and acronym:

advisory.html

Browsers choose how to use advisory information. Here the title is shown as a tooltip in the desktop browser while the Perl acronym is automatically converted to uppercase in the mobile browser.

```
<html>
<head>
   <title>XHTML Advisory Tags</title>
</head>
<body>
<p>You can learn

   <abbr title="Common Gateway Interface">CGI</abbr>
   scripting in
   <acronym
     title="Practical Enquiry and Reporting Language">Perl
   </acronym> with <q>PERL in easy steps</q>

</p>
</body>
</html>
```

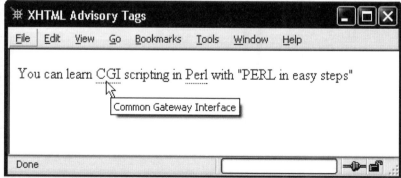

The definition of a term within a XHTML document can be assigned to the **title** attribute of a **\<dfn\>** element. The term itself is contained between the **\<dfn\> \</dfn\>** tags.

Similarly, a citation or reference can be assigned to the title attribute of a **\<cite\>** element.

The example below defines the term 'cybernetics' and uses a **\<cite\>** element to note the location of the web site from where the original definition can be found:

definition.html

```
<html>
<head>
   <title>XHTML Definitions</title>
</head>
<body>
<p>In

   <dfn title="Cybernetics is a science concerned with
   information flow between systems.">cybernetics</dfn>
   , theories tend to rest on four basic pillars: variety,
   circularity, process and observation.
   <cite title="http://pespmc1.vub.ac.be/ASC/
   CYBERNETICS.html">- Principia CyberneticaWeb</cite>

</p>
</body>
</html>
```

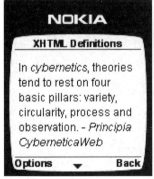

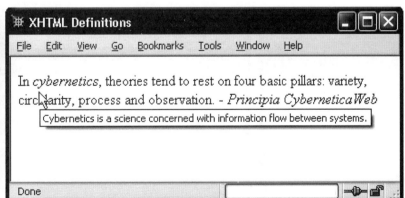

Keyboard input

Where the user is required to enter some keyboard input the text to be entered can be enclosed between **<kbd>** and **</kbd>** tags. The browser may choose to display that text in an enhanced style by default or a stylesheet can define how it should appear.

In the example below the user is asked to enter the word **logout** into a form's text input field, then click a button to exit the page. In this case each browser has chosen to display the text between the **<kbd>** element tags in a small fixed-width font. When the user clicks the button the input entry is submitted to the web server for processing by a CGI script.

keyboard.html

```
<html>
<head>
   <title>XHTML Key Input</title>
</head>
<body>
<form action="http://domain/exit.cgi" method="post">
<p>Finally, type

   <kbd title="Type this to exit">logout</kbd>

to exit, then click the <q>Apply</q> button.<br/>
<input type="text"/>
<input type="submit" value="Apply"/>
</p>
</form>
</body>
</html>
```

Note that the <kbd> tag may optionally include a title attribute. See chapter 10 for more on XHTML forms.

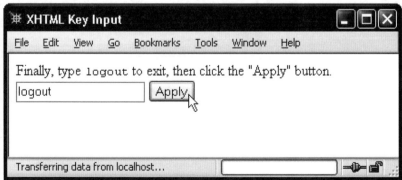

Adding style to content

This chapter demonstrates how stylesheets can be used to suggest how the browser should display various elements of a XHTML document.

Covers

Styling selectors | 50

Styling with class | 52

Styling by identity | 54

Styling spans | 56

Stylesheet efficiency | 57

XHTML colors | 58

Chapter Four

Styling selectors

Cascading stylesheets are useful to specify rules to the browser for how parts of a XHTML document should ideally be displayed. The browser interprets these rules to determine how to display the web page.

Each rule starts by stating a 'selector' that specifies the element to which the rule should be applied. This is followed by a pair of curly brackets { } that contain the actual rule parameters. Each parameter describes a property of the element and a value that should be applied to it. The property and value are separated by a colon and each parameter is separated by a semicolon.

Cascading stylesheet (CSS) parameters identify the property of each element with keywords that are recognized in the CSS language. For instance, a rule for the background and foreground colors of the overall document body can be specified like this:

```
body { background-color: blue; color: yellow }
```

Notice that the final parameter need not end with a semicolon.

A stylesheet rule like this will, by default, 'cascade' down from the parent **<body>** element to all its child elements such as heading, paragraph and division elements.

A XHTML element that contains another element is described as a parent-child relationship – the outer element is the parent to the inner child element.

Additional rules for the document's child elements can be stated in the stylesheet to override those of the parent element. Given that the rule above will create a blue background and yellow text throughout the document an additional rule could be added to the stylesheet to apply a white background and red foreground to each **<h3>** element like this:

```
h3 { background-color: white; color: red }
```

Other rules can also be added to the stylesheet to suggest how each child element should appear.

The many keywords of the CSS language are used to describe each aspect of XHTML elements throughout the ensuing chapters of this book.

In the example on the opposite page stylesheet rules are specified for the document **<body>** element and various child elements.

```
body  { background-color: yellow;   color: blue }

h3    { background-color: white;  color: red }

p     { background-color: lime;   color: black }

div   { background-color: purple; color: yellow }
```

colors.css

colors.html

```
<html>
<head>
  <title>XHTML Stylesheet</title>

  <link rel="stylesheet"
        href="colors.css" type="text/css" />

</head>
<body>

  <h2>Default Colors</h2>
  <h3>Stylesheet Colors</h3>
  <p>This is a paragraph.</p>
  <div>This is a division.</div>

</body>
</html>
```

Styling with class

All the elements that can be contained within a XHTML document body (as described in the previous chapter) can, optionally, include core attributes named **class**, **id** and **title**.

Typically the **title** attribute's value will be displayed in a desktop browser as a tooltip when the user places their mouse over that element in the document.

The **class** and **id** attributes are particularly useful to identify individual elements in a style sheet.

Defining a class rule in a stylesheet enables that rule to be applied to any element within a XHTML document simply by assigning its selector name to the element's **class** attribute.

Prefix the selector name with a dot character to create a class rule.

For instance, a class rule to apply a yellow background and a blue foreground could look like this:

```
.blue-on-yellow { background-color: yellow; color: blue }
```

Then this rule can be applied to a paragraph by assigning its selector name to the element's **class** attribute like this:

```
<p class="yellow-blue"> ... </p>
```

Specifying style rule classes like this is more flexible than stating rules for element types, as in the previous example, because it enables the style rule to be applied to any element.

In the example on the opposite page the style sheet creates a class called **monofont** that suggests the browser should display any element of that class in a mono-spaced font style.

This rule is applied to two different elements in the document.

In this case a single rule is applied to the elements in both desktop and handheld browsers. Different rules for each browser could be specified by including a second **<link>** element and including **media** attributes to assign different stylesheets to each browser. Refer back to the example on page 29 that demonstrates how to apply different stylesheets according to the type of browser.

class.css

```
.monofont
{
  font-family: monospace;
  background-color: yellow;
  color: red
}
```

class.html

```
<html>
<head>
   <title>XHTML Class</title>

   <link rel="stylesheet"
         href="class.css" type="text/css" />

</head>
<body>
   <h2>Default Style</h2>

   <h3 class="monofont">Styled Heading</h3>

   <p>Unstyled paragraph.</p>

   <div class="monofont">Styled division.</div>

</body>
</html>
```

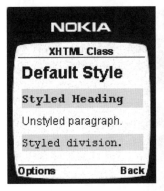

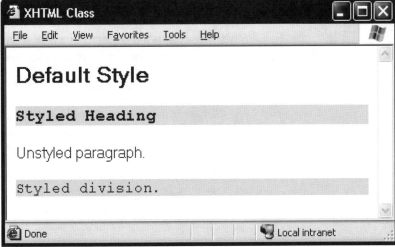

Styling by identity

The greatest control of how individual elements should appear is gained by specifying stylesheet rules using individual element identities as the rule selector.

Prefix the selector name with a **#** hash character to create an **id** rule. Then this rule can be applied to an element by assigning its selector name to the element's **id** attribute.

For instance, a stylesheet rule could be created to centre content within an element with an **id** selector named **central**, like this:

```
#central { text-align: center }
```

This rule can be applied to a single element within a document by assigning that selector name to its id attribute, like this:

```
<p id="central"> ... </p>
```

Whether specifying stylesheet rules by element, **class**, or **id**, a set of rule parameters can be applied to a number of selectors simultaneously by grouping their names at the start of the rule. Each selector name must be separated from the next by a comma. For instance, this example creates a rule for 3 heading elements:

```
h1, h2, h3 { background-color: yellow; color: red }
```

Further control can be added by specifying the name of the parent element before the selector. This means that the rule will only be applied to an element matching that selector name if it is a child of the specified parent element. For instance, the following stylesheet rule is only applied to elements that have a **class** value matching the selector name if their parent element is a **<p>** paragraph element:

```
p.central { text-align: center }
```

A **<div>** element would not be affected by this rule, even if its **class** attribute matches the **central** selector name.

In the example on the opposite page a stylesheet rule is applied to a **<h3>** heading using the **id** selector. The other rule specifies a class. This rule is only applied to the **<p>** element because the rule has the **p** selector before its class name.

id.css

```css
#heading
{
  background-color:red;
  color: yellow;
  text-align: center
}

p.central { background-color:yellow; text-align: center
}
```

id.html

```html
<html>
<head>
   <title>XHTML Identity</title>

   <link rel="stylesheet" href="id.css" type="text/css"/>

</head>
<body>
   <h2>Default Heading</h2>

   <h3 id="heading">Styled Heading</h3>

   <div class="central">Unstyled division.</div>

   <p class="central">Styled paragraph.</p>

</body>
</html>
```

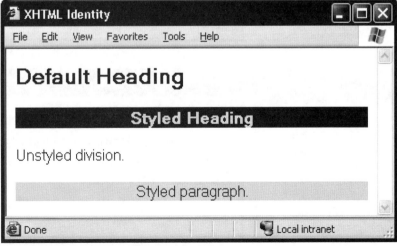

Styling spans

Sections of text, or even a single character, can be defined by the XHTML **** and **** tags. These can optionally include the core attributes **title**, **class** and **id** so that a stylesheet rule can specify how the defined text should appear in a browser.

The example below defines three spans that are each styled individually by the stylesheet:

span.css

```css
#span-1 { font-weight: bold; color: red }

#span-2 { background-color:red; color: white }

#span-3 { font-weight:bold; font-style: italic }
```

span.html

```html
<html>
<head>
   <title>XHTML Span</title>

   <link rel="stylesheet"
         href="span.css" type="text/css" />

</head>
<body>
   <p>The <span id="span-1">Gorge of Samari&agrave;</span>
   on the island of <span id="span-2">Crete</span> is said
   to be the longest gorge in Europe - walking through it
   can take <span id="span-3">4 to 7 hours!</span>
   </p>
</body>
</html>
```

Stylesheet efficiency

It is a good idea to choose a descriptive name for selectors so their purpose is obvious. For instance, the selectors in **span.css,** listed on the opposite page, could be renamed as class rules like this:

site-styles.css

```
.bold-red { font-weight:bold; color: red }

.white-on-red { background-color:red; color: white }

.bold-italic { font-weight:bold; font-style: italic }
```

A browser needs to download a common stylesheet just once – so other pages on that site load faster.

Developing a single stylesheet containing a variety of descriptive style rules allows the same stylesheet to be easily used by all the pages of a website. This is easier to maintain, and much more efficient, than creating separate stylesheets for each page of the site. The XHTML document below uses two of the easy-to-remember selector names in the stylesheet listed above:

site.html

```
<html>
<head>
   <title>XHTML Styles</title>
   <link rel="stylesheet" href="site-styles.css"
        type="text/css" />
</head>
<body>
<h2 class="bold-red">Activities</h2>
<p class="white-on-red">With its magnificent beaches the
major outdoor activity is swimming.</p>
</body>
</html>
```

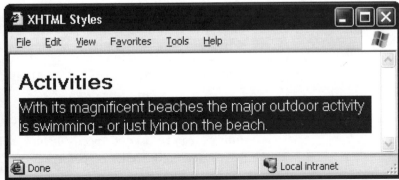

XHTML colors

When assigning colors in XHTML the color can be specified as a six-digit hexadecimal number preceded by a **#** hash character.

This number represents the Red-Green-Blue (RGB) components that make up the whole color. Each of the three pairs of digits can range from 00 (decimal zero) to FF (decimal 255). The first two digits determine its Red component value, the second two digits determine its Green component value and the final two digits determine its Blue component value.

A hexadecimal color number that has all zero RGB values creates Black with the hexadecimal number of **#000000**. Conversely, a hexadecimal color number that has all maximum RGB values creates White with the hexadecimal number of **#FFFFFF**.

To produce a true Red color the hexadecimal value would specify a maximum value for the Red component value and zero for the Green and Blue components – with the number **#FF0000**.

XHTML also recognizes the following 16 colors by name:

Name	Hexadecimal	Name	Hexadecimal
Black	#000000	Green	#008000
Silver	#C0C0C0	Lime	#00FF00
Gray	#808080	Olive	#808000
White	#FFFFFF	Yellow	#FFFF00
Maroon	#800000	Navy	#000080
Red	#FF0000	Blue	#0000FF
Purple	#800080	Teal	#008080
Fuchsia	#FF00FF	Aqua	#00FFFF

Either one of these recognized names, or a hexadecimal color number, can be used to specify a color in a stylesheet rule. This means that **color: red;** and **color: #FF0000;** are both valid rules.

Making lists

This chapter illustrates, by example, how XHTML can be used to display different types of lists in a variety of ways.

Covers

Ordered lists | 60

Unordered lists | 61

Disc bullets | 62

Circle bullets | 63

Square bullets | 64

Decimal bullets | 65

Image bullets | 66

Definition lists | 67

Positioning list items | 68

List style shorthand | 70

Chapter Five

Ordered lists

A list of items, sequentially numbered, can be included in a XHTML document with **<ol>** and **</ol>** tags. Each item in the list must be enclosed between **<li>** and **</li>** tags. All the **<li>** elements are contained within the parent **<ol>** element.

The example below creates an ordered list in which the browser automatically numbers each list item:

ol.html

The numbering style can be changed by a stylesheet rule – see the example on page 65.

```
<html>
<head>
   <title>XHTML Ordered List</title>
</head>
<body>

  <ol>
    <li>Sunday - Kyriaki</li>
    <li>Monday - Deft&eacute;ra</li>
    <li>Tuesday - Tr&iacute;ti</li>
    <li>Wednesday - Tet&aacute;rti</li>
    <li>Thursday - P&eacute;mti</li>
    <li>Friday - Paraskevi</li>
    <li>Saturday - S&aacute;vvato</li>
  </ol>

</body>
</html>
```

Unordered lists

A list of items can be included in a XHTML document without numbering each item using **<ul>** and **</ul>** tags. Each item in the list must be enclosed between **<li>** and **</li>** tags, as with an ordered list.

The example below creates an unordered list in which the browser automatically adds a bullet point at the beginning of each list item:

ul.html

```
<html>
<head>
   <title>XHTML Unordered List</title>
</head>
<body>

  <ul>
     <li>Good morning - kalim&eacute;ra</li>
     <li>Good afternoon - kalisp&eacute;ra</li>
     <li>Good night - kalin&yacute;kta</li>
     <li>Thank you - efcharist&oacute;</li>
     <li>You're welcome - tipota</li>
     <li>Please - parakal&oacute;</li>
     <li>Goodbye - ch&eacute;rete</li>
  </ul>

</body>
</html>
```

Disc bullets

The style of bullet points starting each item in a list can be suggested with a **list-style-type** stylesheet rule. The browser can be instructed to display each bullet point as a filled circle by specifying the **disc** type of bullet point. Typically this may be the default bullet point type but the example below explicitly specifies that **disc** bullet points should be used:

disc.css

```
ul { list-style-type: disc }
```

disc.html

```
<html>
<head>
   <title>XHTML Disc Bullets</title>

   <link rel="stylesheet"
         href="disc.css" type="text/css"/>

</head>
<body>

   <ul>
     <li>Fire - Foti&aacute;</li>
     <li>Police - Astynom&iacute;a</li>
     <li>Ambulance - Asthenof&oacute;ro</li>
   </ul>

</body>
</html>
```

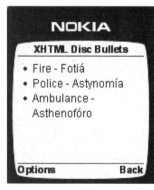

Bullet points are only seen in unordered lists – ordered lists automatically number each list item instead.

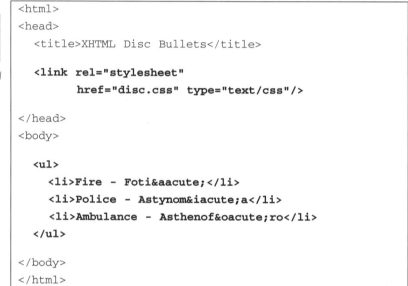

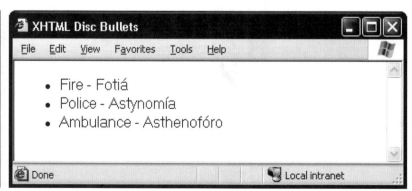

Circle bullets

An alternative style of bullet point can be specified with the **list-style-type** in a stylesheet rule. A **circle** bullet point instructs the browser to display each bullet point as an unfilled circle.

The following example demonstrates how **circle** bullet points begin each list item in a XHTML document:

circle.css

```
ul { list-style-type: circle }
```

circle.html

```
<html>
<head>
   <title>XHTML Circle Bullets</title>

   <link rel="stylesheet"
         href="circle.css" type="text/css"/>

</head>
<body>

   <ul>
      <li>Doctor - Giatr&oacute;s</li>
      <li>Dentist - Odontogiatr&oacute;s</li>
      <li>Hospital - Nosokomio</li>
   </ul>

</body>
</html>
```

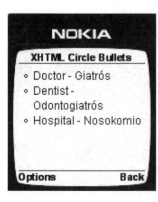

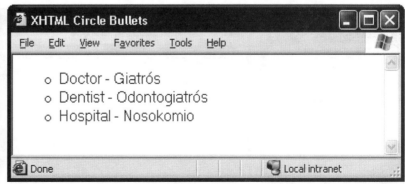

Square bullets

Another alternative style of bullet point can be specified with the **list-style-type** in a stylesheet rule. A **square** bullet point instructs the browser to display each bullet point as a filled square.

The following example demonstrates how **square** bullet points begin each list item in a XHTML document:

square.css

```
ul { list-style-type: circle }
```

square.html

```
<html>
<head>
   <title>XHTML Square Bullets</title>

   <link rel="stylesheet"
         href="square.css" type="text/css"/>

</head>
<body>

   <ul>
     <li>Express delivery - expr&eacute;s</li>
     <li>Airmail delivery - aeporik&oacute;s</li>
     <li>Registered delivery - systim&eacute;no</li>
   </ul>

</body>
</html>
```

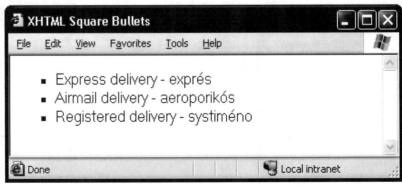

Decimal bullets

Numerical bullet points can be specified in a stylesheet with the **list-style-type** as **decimal**, **upper-roman** or **lower-roman**. Also list items can be lettered alphabetically by specifying **upper-alpha** or **lower-alpha**.

This list example uses the **lower-roman** style of bullet points:

decimal.css

```
ul { list-style-type: lower-roman }
```

decimal.html

```
<html>
<head>
    <title>XHTML Decimal Bullets</title>

    <link rel="stylesheet"
          href="decimal.css" type="text/css"/>

</head>
<body>

    <ul>
      <li>Beer - mia b&yacute;ra</li>
      <li>Bread - psom&iacute;</li>
      <li>Coffee - &eacute;na kaf&eacute;</li>
    </ul>

</body>
</html>
```

The **decimal** type of list style is arabic numbering that is typically the browser's default numbering style.

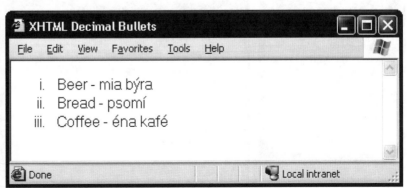

Image bullets

A custom image bullet point can be specified in a stylesheet by stating the location of an image file, in parentheses, after a **url** type to the **list-style-image** rule. The image obviously needs to be of small dimensions like the image file **duke.gif** used in this example:

image.css

```
ul { list-style-image: url("duke.gif") }
```

image.html

```
<html>
<head>

  <title>XHTML Image Bullets</title>

  <link rel="stylesheet"
        href="image.css" type="text/css"/>

</head>
<body>

  <ul>
    <li>Java Program</li>
    <li>Java Applet</li>
    <li>Java Midlet</li>
  </ul>

</body>
</html>
```

The location of the image file can be stated as an absolute address or as a relative address – as seen here.

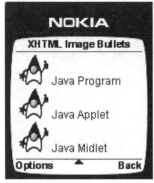

Definition lists

A XHTML definition list is a unique type of list where each list item consists of a term and its definition. All definition list items are contained between outer **\<dl>** and **\</dl>** tags. Each term is surrounded by **\<dt>** and **\</dt>** tags while the descriptions are contained between **\<dd>** and **\</dd>** tags. Browsers choose how a definition list appears but typically a line break is added after each **\<dt>** element and each **\<dd>** element is indented, like this:

def.css

```
dt {font-weight: bold; color: red }
```

def.html

```
<html>
<head>
  <title>XHTML Definition List</title>
</head>
<body>

  <dl>
    <dt>XHTML:</dt>        <dd>Content markup</dd>
    <dt>JavaScript:</dt> <dd>Client-side scripting</dd>
    <dt>Perl:</dt>        <dd>Server-side scripting</dd>
  </dl>

</body>
</html>
```

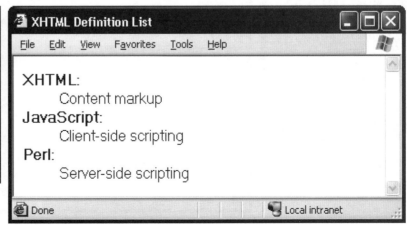

Positioning list items

A stylesheet can indent a list by changing the **list-style-position** from the default value of **outside** to have a value of **inside** like this:

pos.css

```
.sublist { list-style-position: inside }
```

pos.html

```
<html>
<head>
  <title>XHTML List Position</title>

  <link rel="stylesheet" href="pos.css" type="text/css"/>

</head>
<body>
  <ul> <li>Fish</li> <li>Fruit</li> </ul>

  <ol class="sublist">
    <li>Apples</li> <li>Oranges</li> <li>Bananas</li>
  </ol>

  <ul> <li>Vegetables</li> </ul>
</body>
</html>
```

It is not possible to nest a list within another list in XHTML.

Individual list items can be indented by creating a **text-indent** style rule that can be assigned to the **class** attribute of any **\<li\>** element.

This example requests individual list items to be indented a distance of 100 pixels using the abbreviation **px** for pixels:

indent.css

```
.indent-100 { text-indent: 100px;
              list-style-type: decimal }
```

indent.html

```
<html>
<head>
   <title>XHTML Indent Item</title>

   <link rel="stylesheet"
         href="indent.css" type="text/css"/>

</head>
<body>
<ol>
   <li>Fruit</li>
   <li class="indent-100">Apples</li>
   <li class="indent-100">Oranges</li>
   <li>Vegetables</li>
</ol>
</body>
</html>
```

Notice how the item numbering increments even when a non-numeric bullet is used. The Nokia browser only indents a modest amount due to its limited screen size.

List style shorthand

All list styles can be specified with a single **list-style** rule stating the bullet type, position and bullet image location – in any order. This shorthand version replaces separate **list-style-type**, **list-style-image** and **list-style-position** rules. The example below uses shorthand **list-style** rules to suggest how two short lists should appear:

shortlist.css

```
.star { list-style: square outside url("star.gif") }

.moon { list-style: circle inside  url("moon.gif") }
```

shortlist.html

```
<html>
<head>
   <title>XHTML List Shorthand</title>

   <link rel="stylesheet"
         href="shortlist.css" type="text/css"/>
</head>
<body>
   <ul class="star">
      <li>Thursday</li> <li>Friday</li>
   </ul>
   <ul class="moon">
      <li>Afternoon</li> <li>Evening</li>
   </ul>
</body>
</html>
```

The specified bullet type is displayed for the second list in this example because the browser cannot locate its specified bullet image file.

Building tables

This chapter describes the XHTML table model that enables content to be displayed quickly. It demonstrates all the table tags to illustrate how to define rows, columns and cells.

Covers

A simple table | 72

Adding a table caption | 74

Adding column headings | 75

Spanning rows | 76

Spanning columns | 77

Aligning content | 78

Header information | 80

Categorizing cell data | 82

Abbreviated content | 84

Chapter Six

A simple table

Tables are frequently used to display information in XHTML documents and are enclosed between **<table>** and **</table>** tags. Each piece of table data is contained in a cell, defined by the XHTML **<td>** and **</td>** tags, and each row of cells is contained between **<tr>** and **</tr>** tags.

The **<table>** tag may optionally contain a **summary** attribute to which a brief description of the table may be assigned.

The example below creates a simple table specifying a descriptive value to the **summary** attribute:

table-1.html

Later examples in this chapter build on this simple table as more XHTML table features are introduced.

```
<html>
<head>
   <title>XHTML Simple Table</title>
</head>
<body>

<table summary="Simple Table">
  <tr>
    <td>Cell 1</td> <td>Cell 2</td> <td>Cell 3</td>
  </tr>
</table>

</body>
</html>
```

The edge of each table cell can be made visible by adding a **border** rule to a stylesheet. This can specify the width, type and color to be used for each table cell - in any order. The border width can be stated in pixels, using the **px** abbreviation, and an unbroken border type can be defined with the **solid** keyword.

The overall width of the table can be specified in a stylesheet **width** rule – either as pixels, using the **px** abbreviation, or as a **%** percentage of the total available display width.

The example below specifies that the table should use the full available width and adds borders and background colors to the cells of the simple table in the previous example:

table-2.css

```
table { width: 100% }
td { background-color: yellow; border:1px solid black }
```

table-2.html

```
<html>
<head>
   <title>XHTML Simple Table</title>

   <link rel="stylesheet" type="text/css"
         href="table-2.css"/>
</head>
<body>
<table summary="Simple Table">
<tr><td>Cell 1</td> <td>Cell 2</td> <td>Cell 3</td></tr>
</table>
</body>
</html>
```

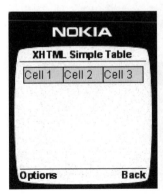

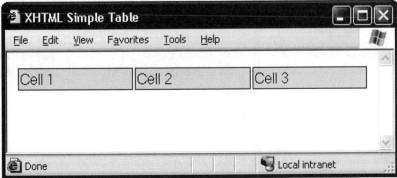

Adding a table caption

A descriptive caption can be added to a table with the XHTML **<caption>** and **</caption>** tags. The browser will determine how to display the caption but a stylesheet rule can suggest how it should be displayed.

The example listed below builds upon the previous example by adding a caption. This has a stylesheet rule specifying white text on a red background.

table-3.css

```
table { width: 100% }
td {   background-color:yellow;   border:1px solid black }
caption { background-color:red; color: white;
          font-weight: bold }
```

table-3.html

```
<html>
<head>
   <title>XHTML Simple Table</title>
   <link rel="stylesheet" type="text/css"
         href="table-3.css"/>
</head>
<body>
<table summary="Simple Table">

<caption>A Simple Table</caption>

<tr><td>Cell 1</td>  <td>Cell 2</td>  <td>Cell 3</td></tr>
</table>
</body>
</html>
```

The browser chooses how to display a caption – here the desktop browser centers the caption text but the Nokia browser does not.

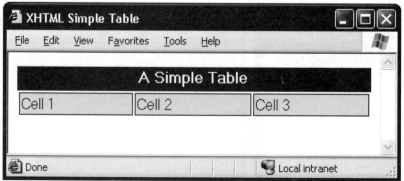

Adding column headings

Headings can be added to each table column with **<th>** and **</th>** tags. These can be identified separately in a stylesheet to make the column headings appear different to the table cells.

This example builds on the previous one to add headings to each column of the table:

table-4.css

```
table { width: 100% }
td {   background-color:yellow;    border:1px solid black }
caption { background-color:red; color: white;
          font-weight: bold }
th { color: blue; border: 1px solid black }
```

table-4.html

```
<html>
<head>
   <title>XHTML Simple Table</title>
   <link rel="stylesheet" type="text/css"
         href="table-4.css"/>
</head>
<body>
<table summary="Simple Table">
<caption>A Simple Table</caption>

<tr> <th>A</th> <th>B</th> <th>C</th> </tr>

<tr><td>Cell 1</td> <td>Cell 2</td> <td>Cell 3</td></tr>
</table>
</body>
</html>
```

HOT TIP

The stylesheet table-4.css listed here is used by all other examples in this chapter.

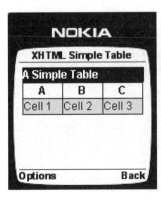

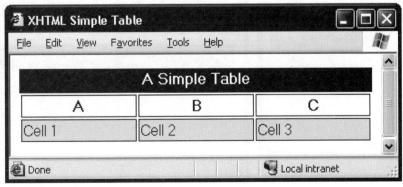

Spanning rows

A table cell can be made to span across multiple rows by adding the optional **rowspan** attribute to the **<td>** tag. This attribute is assigned the number of rows that the cell should span. The cells being spanned in other rows must be removed.

This example builds on the previous example (and uses the same stylesheet) to demonstrate how Cell 1 spans across two rows:

rowspan.html

There is no Cell 4 in this example because its place is being spanned by Cell 1.

```
<html>
<head>
  <title>XHTML Row Span</title>
  <link rel="stylesheet" type="text/css"
        href="table-4.css"/>
</head>
<body>
<table summary="Simple Table">
<caption>A Simple Table</caption>
<tr> <th>A</th> <th>B</th> <th>C</th> </tr>

<tr>
  <td rowspan="2">Cell 1</td>
  <td>Cell 2</td> <td>Cell 3</td>
</tr>

<tr> <td>Cell 5</td> <td>Cell 6</td> </tr>
</table>
</body>
</html>
```

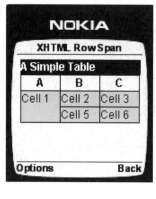

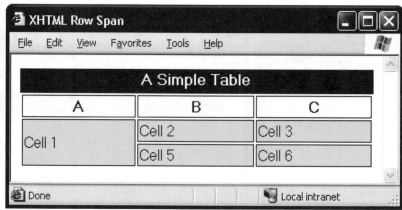

Spanning columns

A table cell can span across multiple columns by adding the optional **colspan** attribute to the **<td>** tag. This works like the **rowspan** attribute and is assigned the number of columns to span. The cells being spanned in other columns must be removed.

The example builds on the previous example to demonstrate how Cell 2 spans across two columns:

colspan.html

```
<html>
<head>
   <title>XHTML Column Span</title>
   <link rel="stylesheet" type="text/css"
         href="table-4.css"/>
</head>
<body>
<table summary="Simple Table">
<caption>A Simple Table</caption>
<tr> <th>A</th> <th>B</th> <th>C</th> </tr>

<tr>
   <td rowspan="2">Cell 1</td>
   <td colspan="2">Cell 2</td>
</tr>

<tr> <td>Cell 5</td> <td>Cell 6</td> </tr>
</table>
</body>
</html>
```

There is no Cell 3 in this example because its place is being spanned by Cell 2.

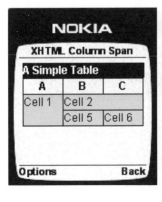

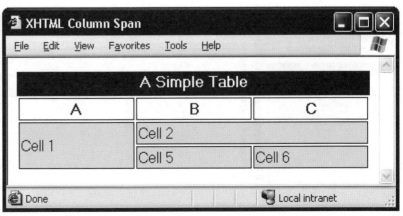

Aligning content

The alignment of content in a table can be specified by adding an **align** attribute to the **<th>**, **<tr>** or **<td>** tags. This attribute can be assigned a value of **left**, **center** or **right** to determine how the browser should display the content.

This example specifies how the text in each table cell should be aligned horizontally:

align.html

```
<html>
<head>
   <title>XHTML Alignment</title>
   <link rel="stylesheet" type="text/css"
         href="table-4.css"/>
</head>
<body>
<table summary="Simple Table">
<caption>A Simple Table</caption>
<tr> <th>A</th> <th>B</th> <th>C</th> </tr>

<tr>
   <td align="left">Left Align</td>
   <td align="center">Center Align</td>
   <td align="right">Right Align</td>
</tr>

</table>
</body>
</html>
```

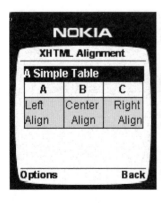

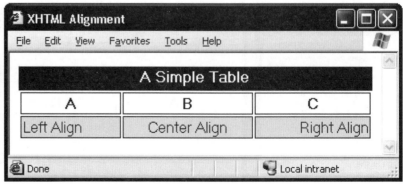

Cell content can also be aligned vertically by adding a **valign** attribute to the **<td>** tag. This attribute can be assigned a value of **top**, **middle** or **bottom** to determine how the browser should display the content.

The example below amends the previous example to display the table's cell content in three different vertical alignments:

valign.html

*Notice that the cell content is centered horizontally by the **align** attribute in the **<tr>** tag.*

```
<html>
<head>
   <title>XHTML Vertical Align</title>
   <link rel="stylesheet" type="text/css"
       href="table-4.css"/>
</head>
<body>
<table summary="Simple Table">
<caption>A Simple Table</caption>
<tr> <th>A</th> <th>B</th> <th>C</th> </tr>

<tr align="center">
   <td valign="top">Top</td>
   <td valign="middle">Middle<br/>&amp;<br/>Center</td>
   <td valign="bottom">Bottom</td>
</tr>

</table>
</body>
</html>
```

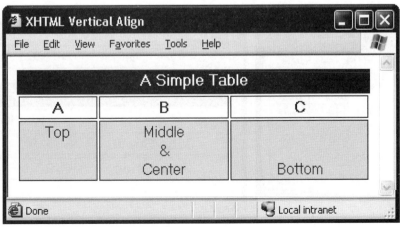

Header information

A **scope** attribute can be added to a **<th>** element to explicitly associate table cell data aligned to that header with a value of **row** or **col** – to associate the aligned row or column. This is useful to implement advanced browser features. For instance, a talking browser could speak the header and cell data of each table cell.

The example below adds **scope** attributes to associate both **row** and **col** cell data to its header cells:

scope.html

```
<html>
<head>
    <title>XHTML Table Scope</title>
    <link rel="stylesheet" type="text/css"
          href="table-4.css"/>
</head>
<body>
<table summary="Employee Ref.No. and Dept">
<caption>Employee Data</caption>
    <tr> <th></th> <th scope="col">Ref.No.</th>
    <th scope="col">Dept</th> </tr>
    <tr> <th scope="row">John Smith</th>
    <td>135-7</td> <td>Works</td> </tr>
    <tr> <th scope="row">Ann Jones</th>
    <td>128-5</td> <td>Sales</td> </tr>
</table>
</body>
</html>
```

This technique is suitable for small simple tables.

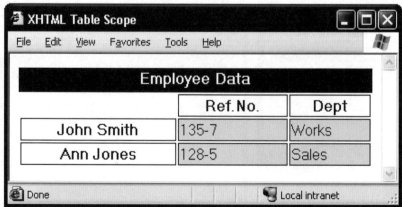

In the previous example each data cell could be associated with both horizontal and vertical headers by adding a **headers** attribute to each **<td>** data cell. Each header can be named by adding an **id** attribute to each **<th>** element. These can then be assigned to the appropriate **headers** attributes as a space-delimited list.

The XHTML document listed below is displayed exactly as before but the **headers** and **id** attributes express the relationship between the table data and multiple headers:

headers.html

```
<html>
<head>
   <title>XHTML Table Scope</title>
   <link rel="stylesheet" type="text/css"
         href="table-4.css"/>
</head>
<body>
<table summary="Employee Ref.No. and Dept">
<caption>Employee  Data</caption>

   <tr>
     <th></th>
     <th id="ref">Ref.No.</th>
     <th id="dept">Dept</th>
   </tr>

   <tr>
     <th id="js">John Smith</th>
     <td headers="js ref">135-7</td>
     <td headers="js dept">Works</td>
   </tr>

   <tr>
     <th id="aj">Ann Jones</th>
     <td headers="aj ref">128-5</td>
     <td headers="aj dept">Sales</td>
   </tr>

</table>
</body>
</html>
```

This technique is suitable for larger tables that are not too complex.

Categorizing cell data

A **<th>** table header element can, optionally, create a data category by assigning a category name to an **axis** attribute. This allows an individual **<td>** table data element to join that category when its **headers** attribute specifies the **id** name of that header.

This technique is suitable for larger complex tables.

A single data cell may join several categories because the **headers** attribute can be assigned multiple headers as a space-delimited list.

In the following example, **axis** attributes are included in the **<th>** table header elements to create categories. All **<td>** table data elements contain monetary values. These become associated to a particular header cell by assigning the header's **id** name to the data cell's **headers** attribute. Each data cell is thereby included in the category created by the **axis** attribute of its associated header.

A talking browser could use this association when the user moved to each data cell. For instance, moving to the cell containing the value **48.50** it could say **"Hotels, 48.50"**, using the associated **axis** attribute value and the data cell contents.

Similarly, moving to the cell containing the value **59.00** a talking browser could say **"Total, Transport, 59.00"**, using the values of both associated **axis** attributes and the data cell contents.

axis.html

```
<html>
<head>
   <title>XHTML Table Axis</title>
   <link rel="stylesheet" type="text/css"
         href="table-4.css"/>
</head>
<body>
<table summary="Accomodation and Travel Report">
<caption>Travel Expenses</caption>

   <tr>
    <th id="header-1" axis="location">Location</th>
    <th id="header-2" axis="date">Date</th>
    <th id="header-3" axis="hotels">Hotel</th>
    <th id="header-4" axis="transport">Transport</th>
    <th id="header-5" axis="subtotals">Subtotals</th>
   </tr>
```

axis.html
(cont'd)

```
<tr>
   <td headers="header-1">Leeds</td>
   <td headers="header-2">25-8-04</td>
   <td headers="header-3">48.50</td>
   <td headers="header-4">27.00</td>
   <td headers="header-5">75.50</td>
</tr>

<tr>
   <td headers="header-1">London</td>
   <td headers="header-2">28-8-04</td>
   <td headers="header-3">67.50</td>
   <td headers="header-4">32.00</td>
   <td headers="header-5">99.50</td>
</tr>

<tr>
   <th id="header-6" axis="total" colspan="2">
     Totals</th>
   <td headers="header-6 header-3">116.00</td>
   <td headers="header-6 header-4">59.00</td>
   <td headers="header-6 header-5">175.00</td>
</tr>

</table>
</body>
</html>
```

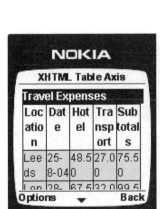

The Nokia browser automatically wraps content to fit the screen – other browsers may provide a horizontal scroll facility instead.

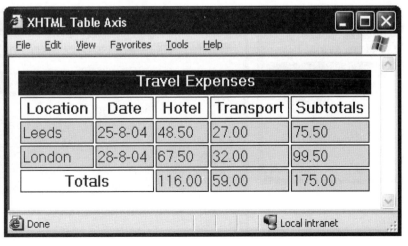

Abbreviated content

All **\<th\>** and **\<td\>** elements may, optionally, include an **abbr** attribute that can be assigned an abbreviation describing the contents of that cell. These will be particularly useful for future speaking technologies that can read row and column labels for each cell. Abbreviations cut down on repetition and reading time.

This example provides a header abbreviation and assigns values to **\<td\>** data cell **abbr** attributes using the standard two-letter language abbreviations described on page 16.

abbr.html

```
<html>
<head>
   <title>XHTML Abbreviation</title>
   <link rel="stylesheet" type="text/css"
         href="table-4.css"/>
</head>
<body>
<table summary="Saying Hello in other languages">
<caption>Saying Hello</caption>
   <tr> <th abbr="lang">Language</th> <th>Hello</th> </tr>
   <tr> <td abbr="fr">French</td> <td>Bonjour</td> </tr>
   <tr> <td abbr="it">Italian</td> <td>Ciao</td> </tr>
   <tr> <td abbr="es">Spanish</td> <td>Hola</td> </tr>
</table>
</body>
</html>
```

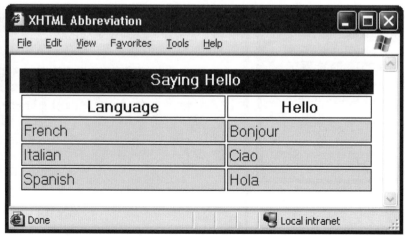

Hyperlinks and anchors

This chapter describes the special ability of XHTML to define hyperlinks that enable users to navigate around the Internet. There are examples showing how XHTML tags can specify content as an anchor or a hyperlink to a variety of targets.

Covers

Creating a hyperlink | 86

Following links | 87

Fragment anchors | 88

Images as links | 90

Setting the tab order | 92

Describing the target | 93

Defining target relationships | 94

Chapter Seven

Creating a hyperlink

Text or an image in a XHTML document can become a hyperlink 'anchor' when contained between **<a>** and **</a>** tags. The destination target of the link is assigned to the **<a>** element's **href** attribute as either an absolute or relative URL address.

The browser displays hyperlinks in a manner that distinguishes them from regular document content. For instance, text that is a hyperlink may be displayed as reverse video, in a different color, or be underlined. Images that are hyperlinks are often displayed with a colored border. In a desktop browser the link destination address is generally displayed in the window's status bar whenever the user places the pointer over the hyperlink.

This example illustrates a text hyperlink that will open a destination document when the user follows the link:

link.html

```
<html>
<head>
   <title>XHTML Hyperlink</title>
</head>
<body>
<p>

Click  <a href="http://localhost/page-2.html">here</a>
to open Page 2.

</p>
</body>
</html>
```

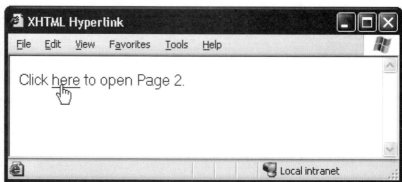

Following links

XHTML provides three means to follow a hyperlink:

Pointer
Use a mouse, trackball or similar device to place a screen pointer over the link then click to load the target document.

Tab
Use a **Tab** key to navigate across the links in a document then hit **Enter** to load the target document. Typically the tab order follows the sequential order in which the links appear on the page.

AccessKey
Use a designated character key (typically 0-9 and #) to focus on a hyperlink then hit **Enter** to load the target document. The character key is specified by adding an **accesskey** attribute to the **<a>** element and pressing that key gives focus to the link.

Accesskeys allow the user to easily navigate links in a long document – add the accesskey number in the regular text to identify the accesskey.

The method of activating the accesskey will vary according to the platform. For instance, Windows users should press **Alt+accesskey** and Mac users should press **Cmd+accesskey**.

The snippet of code below adds an accesskey to the previous example. Activate the accesskey (**Alt+1**) to focus on the link – then hit **Enter** to load the page.

```
<p>
1.<a href="http://localhost/page-2.html" accesskey="1">
Next page</a>
</p>
```

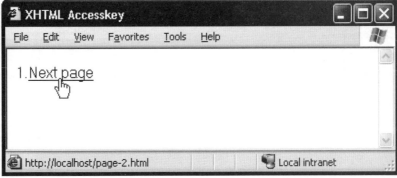

Fragment anchors

Any element can become the target of a hyperlink if its **id** name, preceded by a **#** hash character, is assigned to an **<a>** anchor element's **href** attribute. The **#** hash character denotes that the link's target is an element within a document rather than a URL address – these are known as fragment anchors.

Similarly, a browser can open a document at the precise point at which an element begins if its **id** name, preceded by a **#** hash character, is added onto its URL address. For instance, to open a document at an element with an **id** named **order** the address form of **http://domain/document.html#order** can be used.

It is convenient in long documents to provide a link back to the beginning of the page so that the user need not have to tediously scroll back manually. The following example demonstrates this by including an **id** attribute in the **<h3>** element at the start of the page. The **id** name is assigned to the **href** attribute in the link at the bottom of the page so the reader can easily return to the top.

fragment.html

Notice that the <a> anchor element needs to be contained between <p> paragraph tags.

```
<html>
<head>
   <title>XHTML Fragment</title>
</head>
<body>

   <h3 id="top">History of Crete</h3>

   <p>
      While the rest of the world was still in the Stone
      Age, migrants from Anatolia (Asia Minor), Egypt and
      Libya began a new civilization on the island of
      Crete. This sophisticated culture, now called Minoan
      after king Minos and his descendants, lasted from
      around 3000 BC to 1400 BC. At the peak of their
      golden age the Minoans no doubt considered their
      European counterparts to be total barbarians.
   </p>

   <p> <a href="#top">Top of this page</a> </p>

</body>
</html>
```

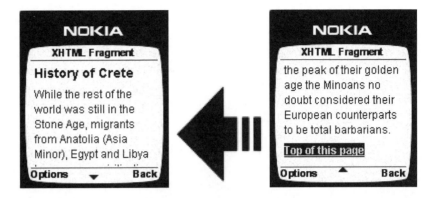

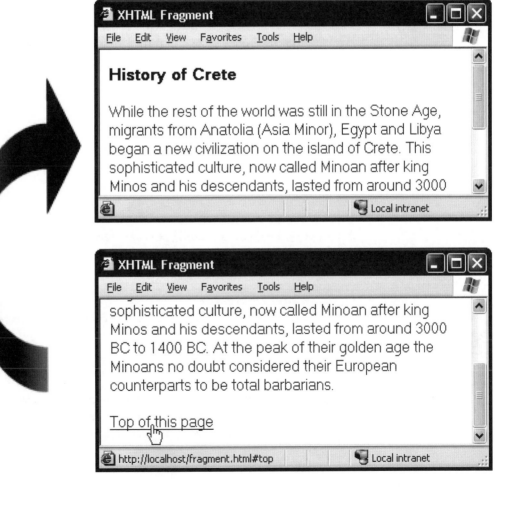

Images as links

Images can be made into hyperlinks by enclosing an **<img>** image element between the **<a>** and **</a>** anchor tags. The image element assigns the location of the image to its **src** attribute. Its **alt** attribute also specifies alternative text to be displayed when the browser cannot display the image for some reason. Additionally, it may also include a **title** attribute that typically displays its assigned value as a tooltip in a desktop browser.

See page 96 for more on image elements.

The document listed below contains three hyperlinks based on the same image. Browsers generally surround each image with a border by default to indicate that the images are, in fact, hyperlinks. These can be removed by adding a stylesheet rule specifying zero border width like this: **img { border-width: 0px }**. However, this should be used cautiously – while desktop browsers indicate hyperlinks by changing the cursor style when the pointer is moved over a link, small-device browsers may have no way to indicate hyperlinks if the borders are removed.

ilink.html

*Use separate stylesheets for **desktop** and **handheld** media to remove hyperlink image borders from desktop browsers only – see the example on page 29.*

```
<html>
<head>
   <title>XHTML Image Link</title>
</head>
<body>
<p>

  <a href="cp.gif">
  <img src="book-icon.gif" alt="book cover image"
  title="Click to view cover shot"/> </a>
  C Programming in easy steps<br/>

  <a href="j2.gif">
  <img src="book-icon.gif" alt="book cover image"
  title="Click to view cover shot"/> </a>
  Java 2 in easy steps<br/>

<a href="cpp.gif">
  <img src="book-icon.gif" alt="book cover image"
  title="Click to view cover shot"/> </a>
  C++ Programming in easy steps<br/>
</p>
</body>
</html>
```

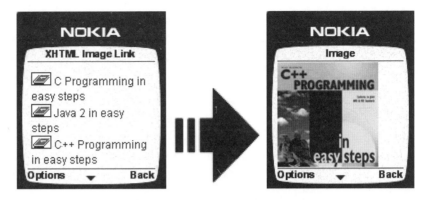

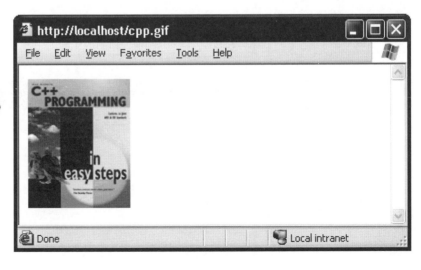

Setting the tab order

A tab key allows the user to navigate sequentially through all the hyperlinks in a XHTML document. Normally the first time the tab key is pressed focus is given to the first hyperlink in that document, the next press moves to the second link, and so on.

The **<a>** anchor element can optionally include a **tabindex** attribute to which numeric values can be assigned to suggest a tab order. The tab key can then be used to navigate through the links in the ascending order of their numeric values. These need not be consecutive numbers but they must be positive values.

A special tab order is created in the example below, allowing the user to navigate the hyperlinks in the order of the target document number, rather than the order in which they appear on the page:

tab.html

*Some devices may not support **tabindex** – these will tab through the links in the order they appear on the page regardless of **tabindex** values.*

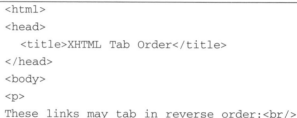

```
<html>
<head>
   <title>XHTML Tab Order</title>
</head>
<body>
<p>
These links may tab in reverse order:<br/>

   <a href="page-3.html" tabindex="3">Link 1</a> -
   <a href="page-2.html" tabindex="2">Link 2</a> -
   <a href="page-1.html" tabindex="1">Link 3</a>

</p>
</body>
</html>
```

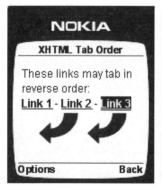

Describing the target

XHTML has three optional attributes for the **\<a\>** anchor element that can be included to describe features of the target document.

See page 98 for more on MIME types.

A **charset** attribute can specify the character encoding of the target page and a **type** attribute can specify its MIME content type. Similarly, the base language used by the target document can be specified by a **hreflang** attribute – this will be one of the recognized two-letter language codes described on page 16.

The example listed below provides a hyperlink to a French version of the current page. The **\<a\>** anchor element attributes set the character encoding to **UTF-8** and describe the target as a HTML document written in the French language.

features.html

```
<html>
<head>
   <title>XHTML Link Features</title>
</head>
<body>
<p>...and so we reach the end of this story.</p>
<p>

  <a href="page-fr.html"
  charset="UTF-8" type="text/html" hreflang="fr">
  This page in French<br/>
  Cette page en Fran&ccedil;ais</a>

</p>
</body>
</html>
```

Defining target relationships

An **<a>** anchor element can, optionally, include **rel** and **rev** attributes to describe the relationship between linked resources. These are used just like the **rel** and **rev** attributes that can appear in a **<link>** element. Both attributes can be assigned one of the descriptive keywords in the table on page 30.

The **rel** attribute defines the relationship from the current document to the target resource, while the **rev** attribute defines the relationship from the target resource back to the current document. This especially is useful when the linked resource is not another document – an image file for instance.

In this example **rel** and **rev** attributes describe the relationship between a home page and three sub-pages:

rel.html

```
<html>
<head>
  <title>XHTML Relationships</title>
</head>
<body>
<p>
  <a href="stories.html" rel="next" rev="prev">Tails</a>
  <br/>
  <a href="photos.html" rel="next" rev="prev">Snaps</a>
  <br/>
  <a href="humour.html" rel="next" rev="prev">Jokes</a>
</p>
</body>
</html>
```

Embedding objects

This chapter demonstrates how to create content-rich web pages by adding diverse content into XHTML documents. There are examples that incorporate other text and XHTML documents plus images, applets, animation and video.

Covers

Adding an image | 96

Objects and MIME types | 98

Embedded image object | 99

Embedded text | 100

Embedded Java applet | 102

Embedded multimedia | 104

QuickTime & Real media players | 106

Flash movie player | 108

Chapter Eight

Adding an image

The **<img>** element is used to insert images into a XHTML document. This is always a single empty tag – so it must end with a forward slash character.

Its **src** attribute specifies the URL address of the image to be inserted into the web page. This can be stated either as a full absolute address, such as **http://domain/image.gif,** or as a relative address for a file in the same directory as the XHTML document, such as **image.gif**.

It is common to place a web site's image files in a sub-directory to that containing the XHTML files. Typically this is named **images**. This sub-directory can be addressed relatively from the XHTML files by prefixing the image file name with **images/**. For instance, a file named **image.gif** within the **images** sub-directory can be addressed from the XHTML document as **images/image.gif**.

Each **<img>** element should always include an **alt** attribute specifying descriptive text that can be displayed by the browser when it is unable, for some reason, to display the image file. For instance, in a text-based browser.

More comprehensive information can be provided for text-based browsers by adding a **longdesc** attribute to the **<img>** element to specify the URL address of a document containing a long description of the image.

The file format preferred by many small-device browsers is the popular Graphic Interchange Format (GIF) although they may not support GIF animation. This format has the advantage of allowing one color to be nominated as transparent – the browser will not display that color.

Image maps (maps that refer to separate areas of an image by their XY coordinates) are not supported in small-device browsers.

An image will normally be displayed to its original dimensions but **width** and **height** attributes can be added to the **<img>** element to specify forced dimensions that the browser should use instead. Small-device browsers may not implement this feature however.

Stylesheet rules can be applied to selected **<img>** elements by adding **id** or **class** attributes, as usual. A **title** attribute allows the image to be named and this is often displayed as a tooltip.

...cont'd

The example below displays a GIF image from the **images** sub-directory. Alternative text is supplied in case the browser could not display the image. A long description of the image is provided in a plain text file for text-based browsers. The **title** text is displayed in desktop browsers when the user rests the pointer over the image.

muto.txt

This image depicts a Mutoscope card. Mutoscope cards were produced in the USA during the 1940s and dispensed by vending machines for around two cents each. They have a distinctive size of 5.25" x 3.25". All Mutoscope cards carry the inscription 'A Mutoscope Card'.

img.html

```html
<html>
<head>
   <title>XHTML Images</title>
</head>
<body>
<p>

<img src="images/muto.gif" alt="Mutoscope Card Image"
 longdesc="muto.txt" title="A Mutoscope Card" />

</p>
</body>
</html>
```

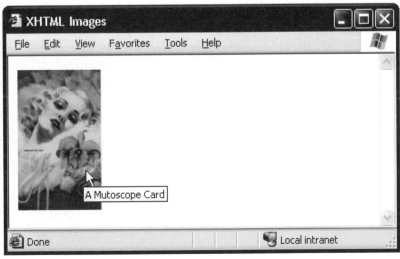

Objects and MIME types

A variety of resources can be embedded into a XHTML document with **<object>** and **</object>** tags. These can optionally include **width** and **height** attributes to specify dimensions of the web page area to be used for the embedded object.

The URL address of the resource can be assigned to a **data** attribute of the **<object>** element and the resource's MIME type can be assigned to its **type** attribute.

A Multipurpose Internet Mail Extension (MIME) is a registered description of a resource that can be universally recognized by all web browsers.

The table below lists some of the MIME types that are most frequently used to describe common resources:

For details of all MIME types see the W3C website at www.w3c.org.

MIME Type	Object Type
image/gif	GIF image resource
image/jpeg	JPG, JPEG, JPE image resource
image/png	PNG image resource
text/plain	TXT regular text document
text/html	HTM, HTML markup text documents
text/css	CSS cascading style sheet
text/javascript	JS javascript script resource
audio/x-wav	WAV sound resource
audio/x-mpeg	MP3 music resource
video/mpeg	MPEG, MPG, MPE video resource
video/x-msvideo	AVI video resource
application/java	CLASS java resource
application/pdf	PDF portable document

Embedded image object

An image may be embedded into a XHTML document by the **<object>** and **</object>** tags.

The URL address of the image file is assigned to the **<object>** element's **data** attribute and the MIME type of the image is assigned to its **type** attribute. The size of the embedded image is specified by **width** and **height** attributes.

Alternative text, to be displayed in the event that the image cannot be embedded into the XHTML document for some reason, can be included between the **<object>** and **</object>** tags.

In this example the desktop browser successfully embeds the specified image. The Nokia browser, on the other hand, cannot embed objects so displays the alternative text.

img-obj.html

All alternative text is completely ignored – unless the object cannot be embedded.

```
<html>
<head>
   <title>XHTML Image Objects</title>
</head>
<body>
<p>

   <object data="lilguy.gif" type="image/gif"
    width="29" height="24">[Lilguy Image]</object>

This is an embedded image object
</p>
</body>
</html>
```

Embedded text

A plain text file can be embedded into a XHTML document with **<object>** and **</object>** tags.

The URL address is assigned to the **data** attribute, as in the previous example, but in this case the MIME type must be specified as **text/plain**.

The example below attempts to embed a text file but usefully provides an alternative hyperlink to that file in the event that the browser cannot embed the file into the XHTML document.

txt-obj.html

```
<html>
<head>
   <title>XHTML Text Objects</title>
</head>
<body>
<p>This is regular text that
<br/>

   <object data="text.txt"
    type="text/plain" width="250" height="70">
   [<a href="text.txt">View contents</a>]
   </object>

<br/>continues around embedded text.
</p>
</body>
</html>
```

The XHTML **<object>** and **</object>** tags can also be used to embed other XHTML documents in a web page by specifying the MIME type as **text/html** to the **<object>** element's **type** attribute.

This next example embeds the XHTML example document on page 74 into another web page.

Notice how the browser automatically provides scrollbars for the area of the embedded object – both in this example and the previous one on the opposite page.

htm-obj.html

```
<html>
<head>
  <title>XHTML HTM Objects</title>
</head>
<body>
<p>This is regular text that<br/>

  <object data="table-3.html"
  type="text/html" width="380" height="100">
  [<a href="table-3.html">View contents</a>]
  </object>

<br/>continues around embedded text.
</p>
</body>
</html>
```

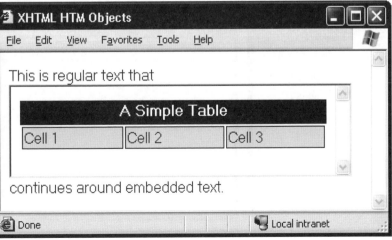

Embedded Java applet

An **<object>** element attribute named **classid** can be used to embed a Java applet into a XHTML document.

The classid attribute is assigned the **java:** protocol specifier followed by the name of the Java class – without any file extension. As usual, the **data** attribute specifies the URL address of the file.

When the **classid** attribute is used the regular **type** attribute should be replaced by a **codetype** attribute to specify the MIME type. In the case of a Java applet the MIME type is **application/java**.

java-obj.html

The alternative text between the <object> and </object> tags will only be displayed when the browser cannot load the applet.

```
<html>
<head>
   <title>XHTML Java Objects</title>
</head>
<body>
<p>This is regular text that<br/>

   <object classid="java:hello" data="hello.class"
     codetype="application/java" width="320" height="73">
     [Java Hello Applet]
</object>

<br/>continues around embedded objects.
</p>
</body>
</html>
```

...cont'd

Java applets that have variable parameters may have their initial values set with the XHTML **<param>** tag. This is always an empty element so must end with a forward slash character. All **<param>** elements must be contained between the **<object>** and **</object>** tags. Parameter names that are recognized by the Java code can be assigned to the **<param>** tag's **name** attribute and an associated value can be assigned to its **value** attribute.

This example sets the value of three Java parameters to specify how a digital clock face will appear on the web page:

java-param.html

Applets are supplied with instructions detailing parameter names and their permissible values.

```
<html>
<head>
   <title>XHTML Java Objects</title>
</head>
<body>
<p>This is regular text that<br/>

   <object classid="java:Clock" data="Clock.class"
     codetype="application/java" width="100" height="40">
     [Java Clock Applet]
     <param name="font" value="Arial"/>
     <param name="fontset" value="361"/>
     <param name="colors" value="0209"/>
   </object>

<br/>continues around embedded objects.</p>
</body>
</html>
```

Embedded multimedia

On Windows systems a Microsoft ActiveX component can be embedded into a XHTML document using an **<object>** element. An audio player is created by assigning its component identifier to the **classid** attribute. Various control parameters are specified to **<param>** elements contained between the **<object>** and **</object>** tags.

This example includes an ActiveX control that embeds a console to play a sound file within the XHTML document:

audio.html

Set *autoStart* to *true* and *playCount* to *2* to play a sound file twice when the document loads. Set the **width** and **height** attributes to zero to hide the control panel.

```html
<html>
<head>
  <title>XHTML Audio Player</title>
</head>
<body>
<p>This is regular text that<br/>

  <object width="250" height="65"
  classid="clsid:6BF52A52-394A-11d3-B153-00C04F79FAA6" >
    <param name="URL" value="sound.wav"/>
    <param name="autoStart" value="false"/>
    <param name="playCount" value="1"/>
    [<a href="sound.wav">Sound File</a>]
  </object>

<br/>continues around embedded objects.</p>
</body>
</html>
```

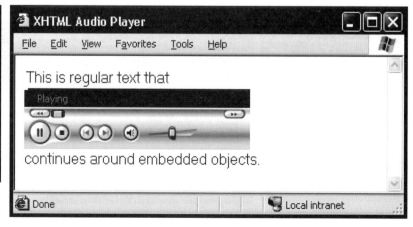

This example embeds the same ActiveX control (but with different parameters) to play a movie file within the XHTML document:

video.html

Notice the **uiMode** *parameter that alters controls – other values are* none, mini *or* invisible.

```
<html>
<head>
   <title>XHTML Video Player</title>
</head>
<body>
<p>This is regular text that<br/>

   <object height="216" width="240"
     classid="clsid:6BF52A52-394A-11d3-B153-00C04F79FAA6">
    <param name="uiMode" value="full"/>
    <param name="URL" value="movie.mpg"/>
    <param name="autoStart" value="false"/>
    [<a href="movie.mpg">Video File</a>] </object>

<br/>continues around embedded objects.</p>
</body>
</html
```

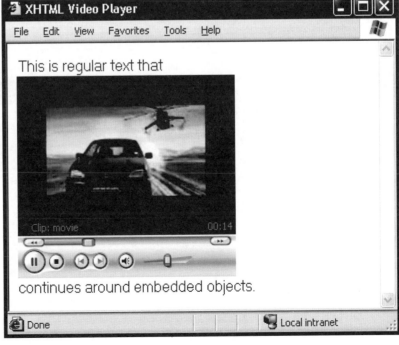

QuickTime & Real media players

A browser plug-in is available from Apple to support their QuickTime media format. Once installed, an ActiveX control is available that can be used to embed a QuickTime media player.

The example below embeds the QuickTime player and adds a **codebase** attribute, stating the location of the plug-in:

qt.html

*QuickTime is the media format favored by Apple Mac users. You can discover more about QuickTime on the Apple web site at **www.apple.com/ quicktime**.*

```
<html>
<head>
  <title>XHTML QT Player</title>
</head>
<body>
<p>This is regular text that<br/>

  <object width="250" height="250" codebase=
   "http://www.apple.com/qtactivex/qtplugin.cab"
    classid="clsid:02BF25D5-8C17-4B23-BC80-D3488ABDDC6B">
    <param name="src" value="sample.mov"/>
    <param name="autoplay" value="true"/>
    <param name="controller" value="true"/>
    [<a href="sample.mov">QuickTime Movie</a>]</object>

<br/>continues around embedded objects.</p>
</body
</html>
```

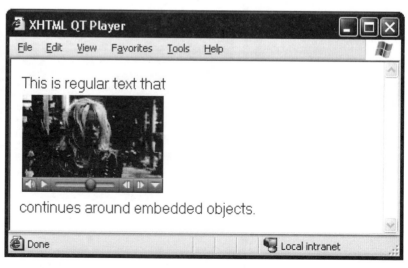

To embed a Real player ActiveX control requires separate **<object>** elements for the **imagewindow** and the **controlpanel**. The values assigned to the **console** parameters must be the same in each case to link the two parts together. The objects look like this:

real.html
(part of)

Real is a high-quality player that enjoys cross-platform support. You can discover more about the Real One media player on the Real website at **www.real.com**.

```
<object id="screen" width="240" height="180"
  classid="clsid:cfcdaa03-8be4-11cf-b84b-0020afbbccfa">
  <param name="src" value="sample.rm"/>
  <param name="controls" value="imagewindow"/>
  <param name="autostart" value="false"/>
  <param name="console" value="one"/>
  [<a href="sample.rm">Real Movie</a>]
</object>
<br/>
<object id="console" width="240" height="36"
  classid="clsid:cfcdaa03-8be4-11cf-b84b-0020afbbccfa">
  <param name="controls" value="controlpanel"/>
  <param name="console" value="one"/>
</object>
```

Flash movie player

Once the Flash browser plug-in is installed its ActiveX control can be assigned to the **classid** attribute of an <object> element to embed a Flash movie player in a XHTML document.

This example plays a Flash movie named **ladybird.swf** that contains an animation. The user can control the direction of movement using the direction keys on the keyboard.

flash.html

*Over 97% of web users have the Macromedia Flash player. You can discover more about Flash on the Macromedia web site at **www.macromedia.com**.*

```
<html>
<head>
  <title>XHTML Flash Player</title>
</head>
<body>
<p>This is regular text that<br/>

   <object id="color" width="250" height="150"
     classid="clsid:D27CDB6E-AE6D-11cf-96B8-444553540000">
     <param name="movie" value="ladybird.swf"/>
     [<a href="ladybird.swf">Flash Movie</a>] </object>

<br/>continues around embedded objects.</p>
</body>
</html>
```

Using frames

The use of frames enables multiple documents to be displayed simultaneously in a desktop browser. Small-device browsers do not support framed pages due to their smaller display area. This chapter demonstrates the display of framed pages in a desktop browser and shows how to provide alternatives for browsers that, for whatever reason, cannot display frames.

Covers

The frameholder document | 110

Two-column frameset | 111

Two-row frameset | 112

Nested frameset | 113

Frame appearance & targets | 114

Alternative content | 116

Chapter Nine

The frameholder document

Frames provide a way to display multiple XHTML documents in a single browser window. This means that some documents can remain on display while others in a different frame are changed.

Typically a window might have three frames consisting of a top banner frame, a left-side menu frame and a main frame containing the changing page content.

The frames could occupy the window like this:

This frame arrangement is demonstrated on page 113.

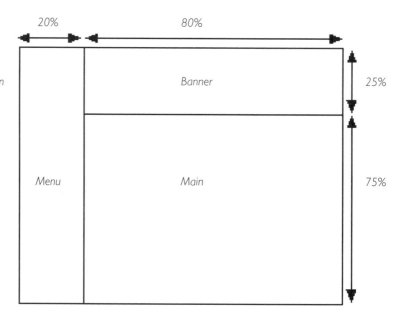

Each frameholder document in this chapter begins with this special frameset DTD.
These are omitted in the listed code examples to save space but must begin actual code in order for it to be valid.

The arrangement of the frames is controlled by the XHTML **<frameset>** and **</frameset>** tags in a dedicated frameholder XHTML document. This contains a **<head>** section and a **<frameset>** section, between the **<html>** and **</html>** tags. It must start with a XML declaration and a special DTD, like this:

```
<?xml version="1.0" encoding="ISO-8859-1" ?>

<!DOCTYPE html PUBLIC
    "-//W3C//DTD XHTML 1.0 Frameset//EN"
     "http://www.w3.org/TR/xhtml1/DTD/xhtml1-frameset.dtd">
```

Two-column frameset

The XHTML **<frameset>** and **</frameset>** tags control the horizontal allocation of frame width with a **cols** attribute.

Values assigned to the **cols** attribute may be expressed either as **px** (pixels) or as a **%** (percentage) – where total width is 100%. The frame values are assigned to the **cols** attribute from left to right as a comma-delimited list. Alternatively a wildcard value can be assigned with a ***** character. This is most useful when the other frames are assigned set pixel values to mean 'the available remaining width'.

The framed documents do not need to contain the special frameset DTD.

The **<frameset>** element contains **<frame>** tags that specify the location of each frame document with their **src** attribute. All **<frame>** elements are empty, so must end with a forward slash.

This example frameholder document arranges the window to display two frames as 20% and 80% of total available width:

twocols.html

```
<html>
<head>
    <title>Two Column Frameset</title>
</head>

<frameset  cols="20%,80%">

    <frame  src="menu.html"/>
    <frame  src="main.html"/>

</frameset>

</html>
```

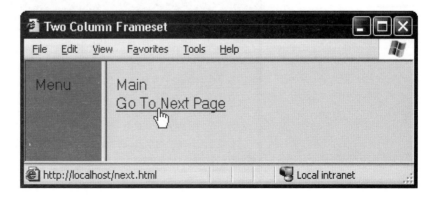

Two-row frameset

The XHTML **\<frameset\>** and **\</frameset\>** tags control the vertical allocation of frame height with a **rows** attribute.

Values assigned to the **rows** attribute may be expressed either as **px** (pixels) or as a **%** (percentage) where total height is 100%.

The frame values are assigned to the **rows** attribute from left to right as a comma-delimited list.

Alternatively, a wildcard value can be assigned with a ★ character. This is most useful when the other frames are assigned set pixel values to mean 'the available remaining height'.

This example frameholder document arranges the window to display two frames as 25% and 75% of total available height:

tworows.html

```
<html>
<head>
   <title>Two Row Frameset</title>
</head>

<frameset  rows="25%,75%">
   <frame src="banner.html"/>
   <frame src="main.html"/>
</frameset>

</html>
```

*Note that this
framest
arrangement
could have used
the wildcard as
rows="25%,*" or (equally)
rows="*,75%".*

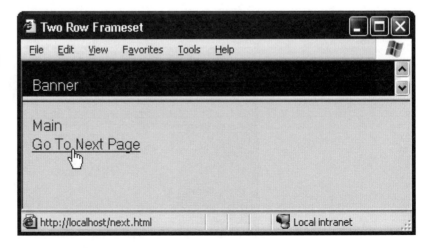

Nested frameset

Frameholder documents can contain nested framesets to provide a more elaborate arrangement of frames.

An initial **<frameset>** could, for instance, assign column widths to two frames. The second **<frame>** could be replaced with a nested **<frameset>** that might then assign row heights to two frames.

This arrangement is illustrated in the example below that creates a window containing a total of three frames:

threeframes.html

```
<html>
<head>
   <title>Nested Frameset</title>
</head>

<frameset cols="20%,80%">

   <frame src="menu.html"/>

   <frameset rows="25%,75%">
     <frame src="banner.html"/>
     <frame src="main.html"/>
   </frameset>

</frameset>

</html>
```

This example combines the previous two examples and follows the frame layout on page 110.

Frame appearance & targets

If a border is not required between frames set the **<frame>** element's **frameborder** attribute to zero. If scroll bars are not required assign a value of **no** to its **scrolling** attribute.

Positioning of the frames contents from the frames edges can be specified by assigning positive pixel values to the **<frame>** element's **marginwidth** and **marginheight** attributes.

A frame's dimension can be made permanent by setting a **<frame>** element's **noresize** attribute to a value of **noresize**.

This example removes all frame borders and the banner-frame scrollbars from the example on the previous page:

noborder.html

```
<html>
<head>
   <title>Borderless Frameset</title>
</head>

<frameset cols="20%,80%" border="0">
<frame src="menu.html" frameborder="0"/>
<frameset rows="25%,75%">
<frame src="banner.html" frameborder="0" scrolling="no"/>
<frame src="main.html" frameborder="0"/>
</frameset>
</frameset>

</html>
```

*Although the **border** attribute shown here is not valid XHTML browser issues may make it necessary to add **border="0"** in the first **<frameset>** to completely hide all borders.*

Hyperlinks normally load target pages in their own frame. A **target** attribute can be added to an **<a>** anchor element in a frameset document to specify which frame should load the target page.

The target attribute can be added to an <a> anchor element in a frameset document – but it is not valid in a XHTML Basic document.

In order to identify the frames each **<frame>** element in the frameset document should include a **name** attribute specifying a unique name. The frame's name can then be assigned to an **<a>** anchor's **target** attribute to load the target document in that frame.

This example assumes that **name** attributes have been added to the frameset on page 113 with assigned values of **menu**, **banner** and **main** respectively. The **<a>** anchor element's **target** attribute specifies that the target page should be loaded in the **menu** frame.

targets.html

The target attribute can be assigned a special value of _blank – use target= "_blank" to load the target page in a new window.

```html
<html>
<head>
   <title>Main</title>
<link rel="stylesheet" type="text/css" href="main.css"/>
</head>
<body>
<p>Main<br/>

   <a href="next.html" target="menu">Go To Next Page</a>

</p>
</body>
</html>
```

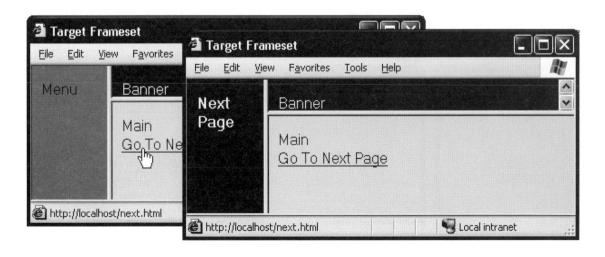

Alternative content

Many people consider that using frames to display multiple documents is bad practice. As the diversity of browsers increases it may be that framed windows are made obsolete.

It is a good idea to provide an alternative for browsers that cannot display frames, or that have their frames facility disabled.

The XHTML **<noframes>** and **</noframes>** tags can be used in a frameholder document to contain content that will be displayed when the frames cannot be loaded. This content must be enclosed by **<body>** and **</body>** tags.

In the example below the Opera desktop browser has frames disabled so the **<noframes>** element offers a hyperlink allowing the user to visit the main page without any banner frame:

noframes.html

Small-device browsers may not display alternative text because they do not support the <frameset> element. A safer option is to provide multiple hyperlinks that give the user the choice of viewing a whole frameset or single frames.

```
<html>
<head>
   <title>No Frames Frameset</title>
</head>
<frameset  rows="25%,75%">

   <noframes><body>This page uses frames -
   <a href="page-1.html">Frameless Version</a> </body>
   </noframes>

   <frame name="banner" src="banner.html"/>
   <frame name="page-1" src="page-1.html"/>
</frameset>
</html>
```

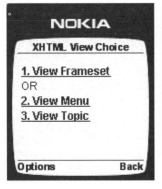

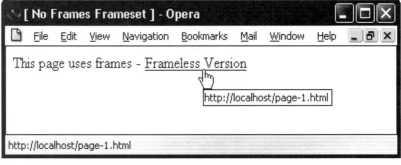

Creating forms

This chapter illustrates how XHTML forms can be used to submit data to a web server. Each type of form element that can interact with the user is demonstrated by example.

Covers

A simple form | 118

Text inputs | 120

Checkboxes | 122

Radio buttons | 124

Selection menus | 126

Text areas | 128

Using labels | 130

Reset buttons | 132

Chapter Ten

A simple form

A submission form is a section of a XHTML document that can contain regular content together with a number of 'controls' which may be modified by the user. Typical controls include text input boxes and radio buttons. The modified form can be submitted to the server where the form controls' input will be processed.

Each control in a form has a **name** and **value** attribute whose assigned values contain the data to be submitted to the server as a series of **name=value** pairs. This is also known as a **key-value** pair.

The term CGI is an acronym for Common Gateway Interface. The CGI form handler used in this example was written in the Practical Enquiry & Reporting Language (PERL).

All form content is contained between **<form>** and **</form>** tags. The **<form>** element must always contain an **action** attribute to specify the location of a form 'handler' that will process the submitted form data. Often the form handler will be a CGI script.

Another attribute of the **<form>** element is the **method** attribute that can specify the type of form submission – as either **get** or **post**. The **get** method appends the **name=value** pairs to the specified form handler's URL address. Unfortunately, the length of a URL is limited, so this method only works if there are just a few form controls. The URL could be truncated if the form contains a lot of controls, or if their values contain large amounts of data. Also, control values appended to the URL are visible in the address field of the browser – not the best place for a password to be displayed.

Form data is sent to the server in an encoded format with a default MIME type of application/x-www-form-urlencoded. *Another encoding format can be specified manually by assigning a different MIME type to an* **enctype** *attribute in a* **<form>** *element – but this is seldom needed.*

The alternative to the **get** method is the **post** method. This method packages the **name=value** pairs inside the body of the HTTP request, which makes for a cleaner URL and imposes no size limitations on the form's output. It also tends to be more secure.

If no method is explicitly specified the **get** method will be used by default – although the **post** method is far more preferable. It is, therefore, a good idea to always include a **method** attribute specifying that the **post** method must be used to submit form data.

The following example posts user input data to a CGI script on the web server when the user activates the submit button. The submitted data comprises a **name=value** pair from a text box and another **name=value** pair from a selected radio button. In this case the form handler is a CGI script that simply echoes the submitted **name=value** data in an output document.

form.html

The **submit** type of **<input>** element displays its assigned **value** on a button.

```
<html>
<head> <title>XHTML Form</title> </head>
<body>

<form  method="post"  action="http://localhost/parser.cgi">
<p>First name: <input type="text" name="username"/> <br/>
<input  type="radio"  name="sex"  value="male"/>Male
<input  type="radio"  name="sex"  value="female"/>Female
<input  type="submit"  value="Submit"/>
</p>
</form>

</body>
</html>
```

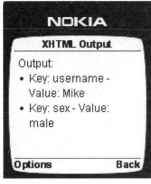

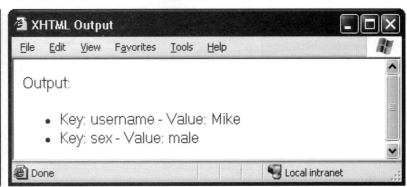

Text inputs

A XHTML **<input>** element that specifies a **text** value to its **type** attribute creates a textbox on the web page which allows the user to enter text for submission to the form handler. The element's **name** attribute must specify a name unique in that form. The entered text is automatically assigned to that element's **value** attribute and the data is submitted as a **name=value** pair.

Each **<input>** element is a single empty element – so must end with a forward slash character.

*Limitation on the amount of text that can be entered is set by the **maxlength** attribute – not the **size** attribute.*

Optionally a **size** attribute can be included to indicate the length of the textbox on the web page. Its appearance is browser-specific so the actual dimensions will vary. Also, a **maxlength** attribute can specify a limit to the number of characters that a user may enter.

This example indicates a textbox **size** and limits the number of characters that may be entered.

text-input.html

```
<html>
<head> <title>XHTML Textbox</title> </head>
<body>
<form action="http://localhost/parser.cgi" method="post">
<p>Zip Code:

   <input type="text" name="zip" size="9" maxlength="5"/>

<input type="submit" value="Submit"/> </p>
</form>
</body>
</html>
```

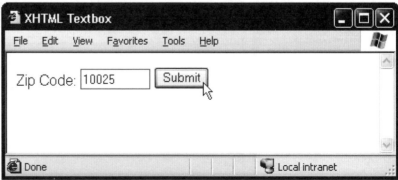

Specifying that an **<input>** element should be a **password** type creates a variation of the standard textbox described in the previous example. This **<input>** element still draws a textbox on the web page but any characters that are entered into that textbox are not displayed literally. Instead each character is depicted in a non-readable format, typically as an asterisk character.

*Using the **get** method to submit a form can briefly reveal the actual **password** in the browser's address field – always submit form passwords using the post method.*

The benefit of the **password** type of input helps to safeguard user passwords by hiding their literal form from other observers. When the form is sent to the form handler on the web server the actual password text value entered by the user is submitted.

All **<input>** elements of the **password** type may also include the **size** and **maxlength** attributes that can be used with **text** inputs.

In the example below a **password** input called login allows the user to enter their password in some privacy:

password-input.html

```
<html>
<head>  <title>XHTML Password</title>  </head>
<body>
<form  action="http://localhost/parser.cgi"  method="post">
<p>Enter  Password:

   <input type="password" name="login"/>

<input  type="submit"  value="Submit"/>  </p>
</form>
</body>
</html>
```

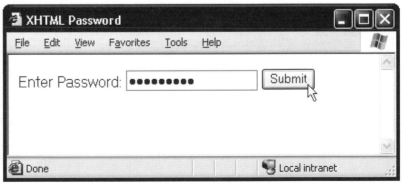

Checkboxes

A **checkbox** type of **<input>** element provides a control that the user can choose to select or ignore. Its specified name and value will only be sent to the web server if that control has been selected by the user.

When the user selects a **checkbox** the browser adds a visual indication to show that it is selected – this can be a tick, a cross, or something else. Avoid using phrases like "tick the box".

Typically each **checkbox** input's **name** attribute is assigned a unique name in the form and its **value** attribute is assigned an associated value. If that **checkbox** control has been selected by the user these will be sent as a **name=value** pair to the form handler when the form is submitted to the web server.

Alternatively several **checkbox** inputs can share a single common name. In this case if more than one **checkbox** is selected each associated **value** is added to the value part of the **name=value** pair as a comma-delimited list.

In the following example the form contains three **checkbox** **<input>** elements but only the first two have been selected by the user. When this form is submitted only the selected controls' values of **coffee** and **cream** are sent in the **name=value** pair and both are associated with the specified **name** of **cup**:

checkbox-input.html

```
<html>
<head> <title>XHTML Checkbox</title> </head>
<body>
<form action="http://localhost/parser.cgi" method="post">
<p>

  <input type="checkbox" name="cup" value="coffee"/>
  Coffee<br/>

  <input type="checkbox" name="cup" value="cream"/>
  Cream<br/>

  <input type="checkbox" name="cup" value="sugar"/>
  Sugar<br/>

<input type="submit" value="Submit"/> </p>
</form>
</body>
</html>
```

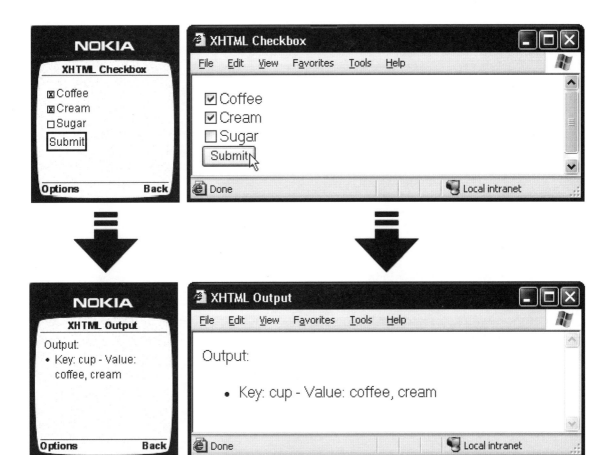

As with hyperlinks, the default tab order of form **<input>** elements is that in which they appear on the page. With the example above, for instance, the default tab order is sequentially from the top **checkbox** down to the **submit** button.

Make a **checkbox** *appear initially* **checked** *if it is a likely option – it saves the user unnecessary effort.*

A different tab order can be created by adding a **tabindex** attribute to each **<input>** element and assigning a numerical sequence.

By default, checkboxes are unselected when they appear on the web page, but they can be made to appear initially selected by including a **checked** attribute in the **<input>** tag. In XHTML, attributes cannot be minimized as they can in HTML so each **checked** attribute must also be assigned the value of **checked**. For instance, to make a **checkbox** initially selected add **checked= "checked"**.

Radio buttons

A **radio** type **<input>** element creates a form control that is similar to a **checkbox**. It may appear singly or as part of a group of **radio** inputs that each have the same name. Unlike the **checkbox** control only one **radio** input can be selected from a group at any given time.

This example sets a radio control to be initially **checked**. Unless a different **radio** input is manually selected by the user this form sends **pop=cola** as a **name=value** pair when this form is submitted to the web server.

radio-input.html

The **radio** control gets its name from old-style radios that had a group of buttons where only one button could be pushed down – push another down and the first one popped back up.

```
<html>
<head> <title>XHTML Radio Button</title> </head>
<body>
<form  action="http://localhost/parser.cgi"  method="post">
<p>

  <input type="radio" name="pop" value="lemonade"/>
  Lemonade<br/>

  <input type="radio" name="pop" value="cola"
    checked="checked"/>Cola<br/>

  <input type="radio" name="pop" value="orange"/>
  Orange<br/>

<input type="submit" value="Submit"/> </p>
</form>
</body>
</html>
```

Hidden inputs

A **hidden** type of **<input>** can be used to send data to the server in addition to user-entered data. This could be useful to identify the XHTML document's URL to the server. For instance, the **hidden** input listed below could be added to the form in the previous example to note the URL of the submitting page:

```
<input type="hidden" name="URL"
       value="http://localhost/hidden-input.html"/>
```

hidden-input.html

The modified example is renamed and its title changed to reflect the addition. Now each time the form is submitted from this new document it will automatically send its URL address details in addition to the selected **radio** input's data:

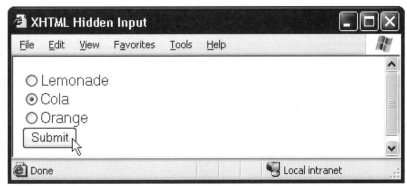

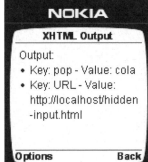

Selection menus

The XHTML **<select>** and **</select>** tags are used to create a menu of selectable options in a form. The **<select>** element must contain a name attribute that specifies a name for the menu. It may also optionally contain a **size** attribute to indicate how many of the menu options should be displayed in a drop-down list.

Each option is defined in individual **<option>** elements that are contained between the **<select>** and **</select>** tags. All **<option>** elements must have a **value** attribute specifying a value to be associated with the **name** attribute in the **<select>** tag. When the form is submitted the menu **name** and selected option's **value** are sent as a **name=value** pair to the web server.

The text to be displayed for a menu item is contained between the **<option>** and **</option>** tags but this is only descriptive – it is the data assigned to its **value** attribute which is submitted when the user activates the form's **submit** button.

The following example creates a menu of airport abbreviations:

select-options.html

The **size** attribute
is ignored by the
Nokia browser in
this example – it
simply lists all the
available options.

```
<html>
<head>  <title>XHTML Select Options</title>  </head>
<body>
<form  action="http://localhost/parser.cgi"  method="post">
<p>

<select  name="city"  size="4">

    <option  value="LHR"  selected="selected">London</option>
    <option  value="NYC">New York</option>
    <option  value="PAR">Paris</option>
    <option  value="LAX">Los Angeles</option>
    <option  value="SYD">Sydney</option>

</select>

<input  type="submit"  value="Submit"/>

</p>
</form>
</body>
</html>
```

Options normally appear unselected but a single **<option>** element can be made to appear initially selected by including a **selected** attribute, that is also assigned the value of **"selected"**. In this case the option for London is initially selected. When the user selects another option the previous selection becomes unselected.

The XHTML specifications also provide an optional **multiple** attribute for the **<select>** element. This can be assigned the value of **"multiple"** to allow the user to select more than one option – but this feature is not implemented by all browsers.

With this example the user might select the option for New York before submitting the form so that **city=NYC** is sent to the server as a **name=value** pair, as seen below:

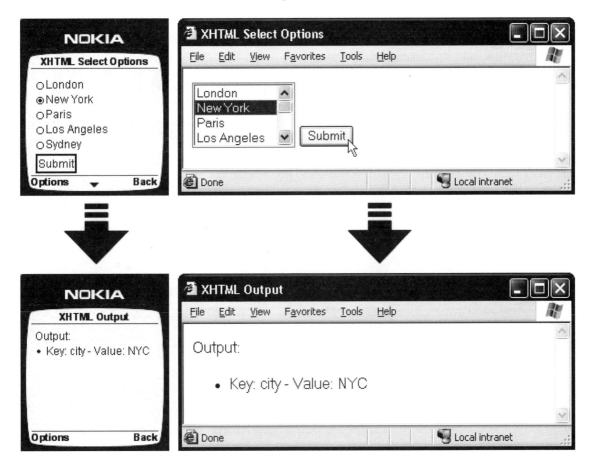

Text areas

For longer texts a **<textarea>** element is often more suitable than using a **text** type of **<input>** element to create a small textbox. The **<textarea>** tag must include a **rows** attribute and a **cols** attribute to suggest what size the area should be.

The **rows** attribute specifies the area's height according to the height of each row of text determined by the browser. Similarly, the **cols** attribute specifies the area's width according to the width of each character determined by the browser.

The browser will normally provide a means for the user to scroll to any text that overflows the text area.

The **<textarea>** tag should also include a **name** attribute to specify a name for that text area. An initial text message can be added between the **<textarea>** and **</textarea>** tags. This can then be replaced by the user's own text entry.

When the form is submitted by the users the **name** of the text area, and the contents **value** of the text area, are sent to the server as a **name=value** pair.

The following example supplies an initial **<textarea>** message that is replaced by the user before submission to the web server. Notice that the initial text is inset by two character spaces in the listed code and this is repeated in the initial **<textarea>** message – space characters are included as part of the text.

textareas.html

```
<html>
<head> <title>XHTML Textareas</title> </head>
<body>
<form action="http://localhost/parser.cgi" method="post">
<p>

  <textarea name="msg" rows="4" cols="25">
  Please leave your message here.
  </textarea>

<input type="submit" value="Submit"/>
</p>
</form>
</body>
</html>
```

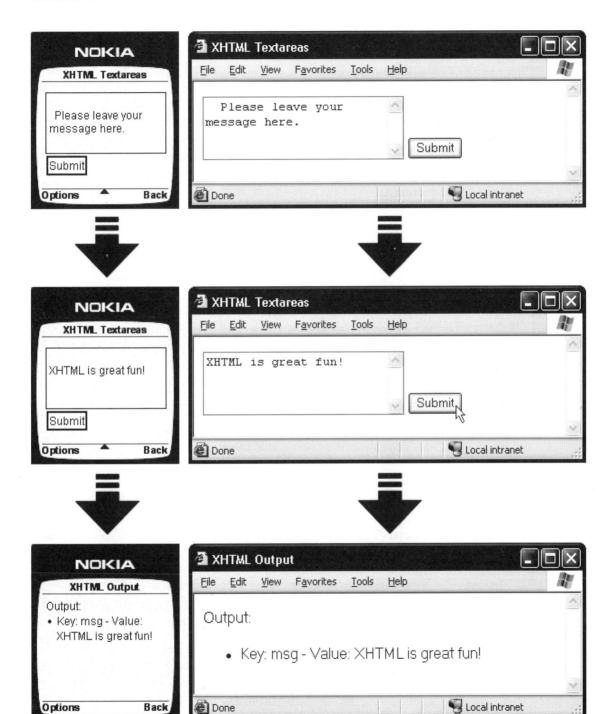

Using labels

The XHTML **<label>** element is useful to specify a text label for form **<input>** and **<select>** elements. This element can be used in two different ways.

The simplest way to use a **<label>** element is to enclose the label text and the **<input>** or **<select>** element between **<label>** and **</label>** tags. For instance, the code snippet listed below adds the text label 'Enter text:' to a **text** type **<input>** element:

```
<label>
Enter text:<input type="text" name="txt"/>
</label>
```

The input label looks like this: Enter text:[   ]

The specific association of labels with *<input>* and *<select>* elements may allow better formatting in future browsers – it's a good idea to get into the habit of using this method now.

A better way to use a **<label>** element allows a specific association to be declared between the label and the **<input>** element. This requires a **for** attribute to be added to the **<label>** tag and an **id** attribute to be added to the **<input>** tag. Now the value of the **<input>** element's **id** attribute can also be assigned to the **<label>** element's **for** attribute to make the association.

For instance, the code snippet shown above could be modified to declare a specific association between the two elements like this:

```
<label for="txt-box">Enter text:</label>
<input id="txt-box" type="text" name="txt"/>
```

This label looks just as before: Enter text:[   ]

Notice how the modified version produces code that is cleaner in appearance. Adding an **id** attribute to any form element also allows stylesheet rules to be applied to that element.

In this example each **<input>** element has an associated label. The **id** attributes are included in every **<input>** and **<label>** element which also allows stylesheet rules to be applied to the labels. The user has selected the **radio** button with a **blue** value, so on submission of the form **fav=blue** is sent as the **name=value** pair:

label.css

```
p { background-color: yellow }
label { font-weight: bold }
#rl   { color: red }
#gl   { color: green }
#bl   { color: blue }
```

label.html

```
<html>
<head> <title>XHTML Form Labels</title>
<link rel="stylesheet" type="text/css" href="label.css"/>
</head>
<body>
<form action="http://localhost/parser.cgi" method="post">
<p>

<input id="rb" type="radio" name="fav" value="red"/>
<label id="rl" for="rb">Red</label> <br/>

<input id="gb" type="radio" name="fav" value="green"/>
<label id="gl" for="gb">Green</label> <br/>

<input id="bb" type="radio" name="fav" value="blue"/>
<label id="bl" for="bb">Blue</label> <br/>

<label id="ol" for="ot">Other [please enter]</label>
<input id="ot" type="text" name="fav"/>

<input id="sb" type="submit" value="Submit"/> </p>
</form>
</body>
</html>
```

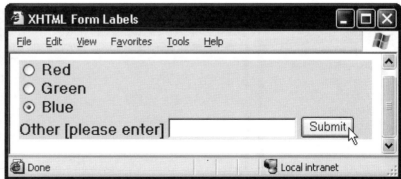

Reset buttons

It is good practice to provide a **reset** button in each form to allow the user to easily return all form fields to their initial state. This is simply an **<input>** element of the type **reset**. Whatever is assigned to the element's **value** attribute appears on the face of the button.

The **reset** button in this example returns all the form's **radio** buttons to their initial **checked** state with just one push:

reset.html

```
<html>
<head> <title>XHTML Reset Buttons</title> </head>
<body>
<form action="http://localhost/parser.cgi" method="post">
<p>Coffee:
<input name="drink" type="radio" value="coffee"/>Regular
<input name="drink" type="radio" value="tea"
   checked="checked"/>Decaffeinated <br/>Milk/Cream:
<input name="with" type="radio" value="none"/>None
<input name="with" type="radio" value="cream"/>Cream
<input name="with" type="radio" value="milk"
   checked="checked"/>Milk <br/>Sugar:
<input name="sugar" type="radio" value="0"/>None
<input name="sugar" type="radio" value="1"
   checked="checked"/>One
<input name="sugar" type="radio" value="2"/>Two<br/>
<input type="submit" value="Submit"/>
<input type="reset" value="Reset"/> </p>
</form>
</body>
</html>
```

*Notice how the line wrap on small-device browsers can often separate a **radio** button from its label. List the radio buttons vertically for better display.*

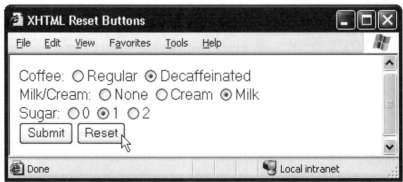

Borders and margins

This chapter describes the components comprising blocks of XHTML document content. Examples demonstrate how style rules can be used to manipulate each component.

Covers

The content box | 134

Background & border color | 135

Border styles & width | 136

Border shorthand | 138

Adding padding | 139

Relative padding | 140

Padding shorthand | 141

Setting margins | 142

Margin shorthand | 143

Putting it together | 144

Chapter Eleven

The content box

Each block of document content is placed onto the page in an invisible content box.

The content box has three properties that may, optionally, specify how the block of content should appear.

Content boxes have a top, bottom, left and right property that can each be addressed individually.

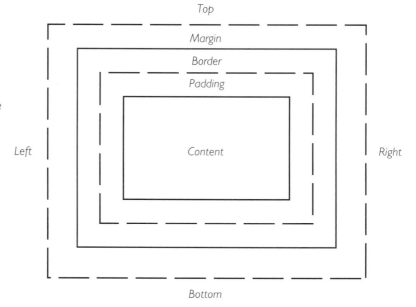

A **padding** property defines the edges of the content box. With a padding width of zero the content box edges are identical to the contained content edges. The content box edges extend as the padding width is increased.

A **border** property defines the width of the area immediately surrounding the content box. With a border width of zero the border edges remain identical to the content box edges. The border edges extend as the border width is increased.

A **margin** property defines the width of the area that immediately surrounds the border edges. With a margin width of zero the margin edges remain identical to the border edges. The margin edges extend as the margin width is increased.

Background & border color

To create a border around a block of content it is necessary to specify its border properties of color, width and style.

The stylesheet **border-color** rule sets the color of the entire content box border. Similarly, its width can be set with a stylesheet **border-width** rule and its style can be set with a **border-style** rule.

A border-width rule can alternatively be set as thick or thin.

The example below initially sets all content box borders to **black** with a width of **25px** (pixels) and drawn in a **solid** style. A **background-color** rule sets the content box's background to **silver**. Top and bottom borders are set individually to **gray**, thereby superseding the general border color rule for those borders.

border-bg.css

```
p { border-color:black; border-width: 25px;
      border-style: solid; background-color: silver;
      border-top-color:gray; border-bottom-color: gray }
```

border-bg.html

```
<html>
<head>
    <title>XHTML Borders</title>

    <link rel="stylesheet" type="text/css"
      href="border-bg.css"/>

</head>
<body>
<p>Content</p>
</body>
</html>
```

Notice how the browsers render the borders in a different way.

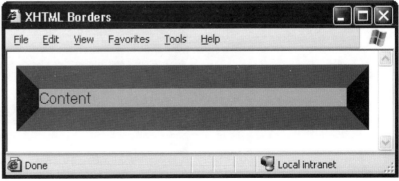

Border styles & width

The style for all four borders around a content box may be set collectively with the stylesheet **border-style** rule.

Alternatively, each border can be set individually with the **border-style-top**, **border-style-bottom**, **border-style-left** and **border-style-right** rules.

Each of the possible border styles are illustrated below but some small-device browsers may not implement all these styles.

To hide any border set its **border-style** *rule to* **none**.

The Nokia browser draws no border at all for the Groove, Ridge, Inset and Outset styles. It only draws a **solid** *border for all the other styles. The Openwave browser draws a* **solid** *border for all styles.*

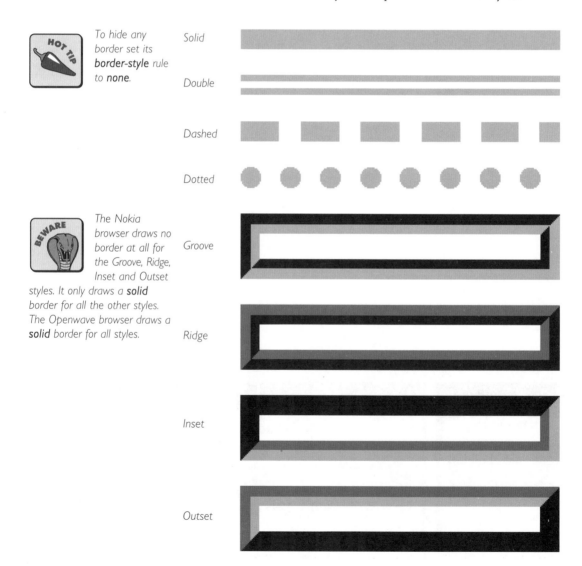

Solid

Double

Dashed

Dotted

Groove

Ridge

Inset

Outset

The width of all four borders around a content box may be set collectively using a stylesheet **border-width** rule.

Alternatively, the width of each border can be set individually with **border-width-top**, **border-width-bottom**, **border-width-left** and **border-width-right** rules.

This example sets a uniform **border-width** for the **silver** border around the first paragraph, drawn in a **dashed** style. Individual **border-width** rules are set for the **black** border around the second paragraph, drawn in a **double** style.

border-w.css

```
#p1 { border-color: silver; border-style: dashed;
      border-width:6px }

#p2 { border-color: black; border-style: double;
      border-top-width:3px; border-bottom-width: 20px }
```

border-w.html

```
<html>
<head>
   <title>XHTML Borders</title>

   <link rel="stylesheet" type="text/css"
     href="border-w.css"/>

</head>
<body>
<p id="p1">Content</p> <p id="p2">Content</p>
</body>
</html>
```

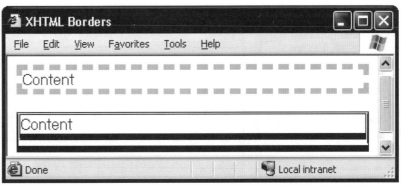

Border shorthand

The order in which the three property values are listed is unimportant.

A single stylesheet rule called simply **border** may be used to specify all the required rules to define a content box border. This shorthand version can only be used when all four borders are to have the same appearance. The **border** rule collectively sets values for a border's width, style and color with this syntax:

```
border: border-width border-style border-color ;
```

In the example below the borders around the first content box are set with individual rules. The second content box's borders appear identical to those of the first content box but these have been set using the shorthand **border** rule.

border-s.css

```
#p1 { border-width: 6px; border-style: dashed;
      border-color: blue }

#p2 { border: 6px dashed blue }
```

border-s.html

```
<html>
<head>
   <title>XHTML Borders</title>

   <link rel="stylesheet" type="text/css"
     href="border-s.css"/>

</head>
<body>
<p id="p1">Content</p>  <p id="p2">Content</p>
</body>
</html>
```

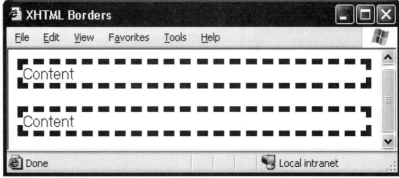

Adding padding

The padding area around the actual content in a content box can be specified with stylesheet rules. This allows control over the space between the content and where the borders will appear.

Individual padding distances can be specified with **padding-top**, **padding-bottom**, **padding-left** and **padding-right** rules.

In the example below a **border** and **background-color** is first set by stylesheet rules. Then **padding-top** and **padding-bottom** rules add 5 px (pixels) above and below the content text. The second paragraph just adds 20px above the content text with a **padding-top** rule.

padding.css

```
p { border: thin solid black; background-color: silver }
#p1 { padding-top: 5px; padding-bottom: 5px }
#p2 { padding-top: 20px }
```

padding.html

```
<html>
<head>
    <title>XHTML Padding</title>

    <link rel="stylesheet" type="text/css"
      href="padding.css"/>

</head>
<body>
<p id="p1">Content</p>  <p id="p2">Content</p>
</body>
</html>
```

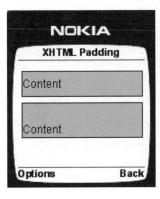
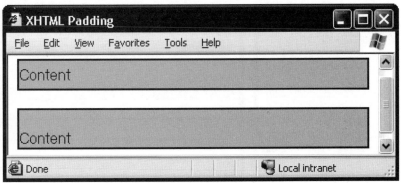

Relative padding

Padding areas in a content box can alternatively be specified relative to other aspects of the document.

*The **em** suffix is a unit value equivalent to the size of the current font.*

They may be specified as a **%** percentage of the block in which they are contained or **em** relative to the current size of font.

This example applies padding twice the width of the current font then 40% of the surrounding content box:

rel-padding.css

```
p { border: thin solid black; background-color: silver }
#p1 { font-size: 8pt; padding-left: 2em }
#p2 { font-size: 14pt; padding-left: 2em }
#p3 { padding-left: 40% }
```

rel-padding.html

```
<html>
<head>
  <title>XHTML Padding</title>

  <link rel="stylesheet" type="text/css"
    href="rel-padding.css"/>

</head>
<body>
  <p id="p1">Content</p>
  <p id="p2">Content</p>
  <p id="p3">Content</p>
</body>
</html>
```

Font size cannot be controlled by stylesheet rules in the Nokia browser so the applied padding is identical in the first and second paragraphs.

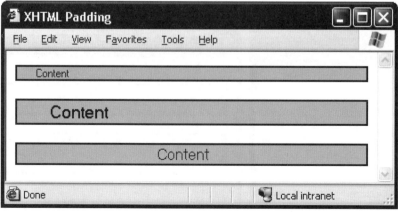

Padding shorthand

A single stylesheet rule called simply **padding** may be used to specify all the rules to define the padding spacing in a content box. It may be used to set padding values for top, bottom, left and right.

If only one value is specified by the rule it applies to all four sides. If two values are specified the first pads the top and bottom and the second pads the left and right. If three values are specified the first pads the top, the second pads left and right and the third pads the bottom. If four values are specified they are applied, in sequence, to the top, right, bottom and left of the content box.

This example uses the shorthand **padding** rule to pad the top, bottom and left areas of a content box:

padding-s.css

```
/* paddings -    top   right bottom   left */
p { padding:    10px  0px    20px    50px;
      border: thick solid black; background-color: silver }
```

padding-s.html

```
<html>
<head>
   <title>XHTML Padding</title>

   <link rel="stylesheet" type="text/css"
     href="padding-s.css"/>

</head>
<body>
<p>Content</p>
</body>
</html>
```

Paragraphs extend across the full width of the page so the area to the right of the content is automatically filled.

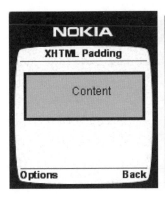

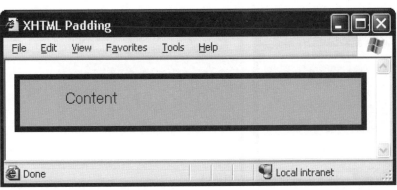

Setting margins

Margin areas, surrounding a content box's padding and border areas, can be specified individually with **margin-top**, **margin-bottom**, **margin-left** and **margin-right** stylesheet rules.

The example below begins by removing any default **margin** in the document body to ensure that first **<div>** element's top left corner is positioned at the extreme top left of the display area. A second nested **<div>** element is positioned offset by 10 px (pixels) and immediately below the content of the first <div> element.

margins.css

```
body {margin-top: 0px; margin-left: 0px }
#d1 { margin-top: 0px; margin-left: 0px; width: 200px;
      height: 75px; background-color: gray }
#d2 { margin-top: 0px; margin-left: 10px;
      width:100px; background-color: silver }
```

margins.html

```
<html>
<head>
   <title>XHTML Margins</title>

   <link rel="stylesheet" type="text/css"
     href="margin.css"/>

</head>
<body>
<div id="d1">Content
   <div id="d2"><p>Content</p></div>
</div>
</body>
</html>
```

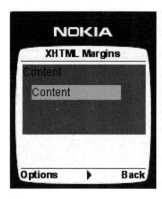

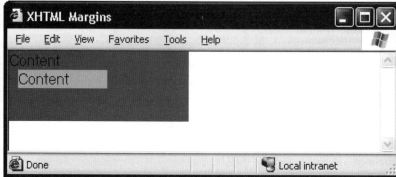

Margin shorthand

A single stylesheet rule called simply **margin** may be used to specify all the rules to define the margins around a content box.

If only one value is specified by the rule it applies to all four sides. If two values are specified the first sets top and bottom margins and the second sets left and right. If three values are specified the first sets the top margin, the second sets left and right and the third sets the bottom. If four values are specified they are applied, in sequence, to the top, right, bottom and left margins.

This example uses the shorthand **margin** rule to set margins for the content boxes contained in two **<div>** elements:

margin-s.css

```
div { border: thick solid black; width: 50px }
#d1 { margin: 0px 0px 0px 20px }
#d2 { margin: 30px 0px 0px 50px }
```

margin-s.html

The second content is positioned 30 pixels below the bottom of the first content box – not 30 pixels from the top of the display area.

```
<html>
<head>
   <title>XHTML Margins</title>

   <link rel="stylesheet" type="text/css"
     href="margin-s.css"/>

</head>
<body>
   <div id="d1">Content</div>
   <div id="d2">Content</div>
</body>
</html>
```

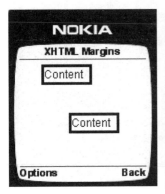

Putting it together

Setting stylesheet rules for a content box's **border**, **padding** and **margin** properties allows a great degree of control over how the content should be presented.

The example listed below combines all the examples listed throughout this chapter by setting a rule for the document's body **border** and rules for the paragraph's **border**, **padding** and **margin** properties. Note that the shorthand version is used for each rule.

together.css

```
body { border: 8px solid gray }

p { border: dotted 3px black;
    padding: 5px;
    margin: 5px;
    background-color: silver }
```

together.html

```
<html>
<head>
   <title>XHTML Border & Margin</title>

   <link rel="stylesheet" type="text/css"
   href="together.css"/>

</head>
<body>
   <h3>Borders are fun...</h3>
   <p>If used in moderation!</p>
</body>
</html>
```

Notice here how Internet Explorer moves the scroll bar inside the content box border – other browsers do not.

Displaying content

This chapter demonstrates how to control content in a web page. Examples show how to make text flow around graphics and how to specify whether items should be visible or invisible. The control of content visibility illustrates how to create a web page which will only display content appropriate for the type of browser viewing that page.

Covers

Block display | 146

Inline display | 147

Electing not to display content | 148

Wrapping text around images | 150

Hiding content | 152

Disallow wrapping | 154

Chapter Twelve

Block display

Some XHTML elements, such as headings and paragraphs, are displayed by browsers as a **block** of content – but other elements, such as spans and cites, are displayed **inline** within those blocks.

This default style can be overridden by explicitly specifying if the content should be displayed as a **block** or **inline** with a stylesheet **display** rule.

This example overrides the default browser setting to **display** the contents of a span element as a **block** of text:

block.css

```
#p1 { background-color: red; color: white }

#s1 { display: block;
      background-color: yellow; color: black }
```

block.html

```
<html>
<head>
  <title>XHTML Block Display</title>
  <link rel="stylesheet" type="text/css"
    href="block.css"/>
</head>
<body>
<p id="p1">This is a block of text <span id="s1">This is
another block of text</span> that has another block of
text nested inside.</p>
</body>
</html>
```

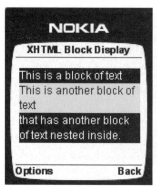

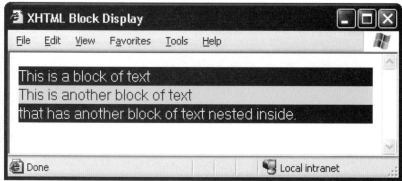

Inline display

In contrast to the previous example on the opposite page elements that are normally displayed as a **block** of content, such as headings and paragraphs, can be forced to be displayed as **inline** content.

Setting a stylesheet **display** rule to **inline** will override the default style used by the browser to ensure that content in the nominated element is no longer displayed as a **block**.

This example overrides the default browser setting to **display** the contents of a paragraph element as **inline** text:

inline.css

```
#p1 { display: inline;
      background-color: red; color: white }

#s1 { background-color: yellow; color: black }
```

inline.html

```
<html>
<head>
  <title>XHTML Inline Display</title>
  <link rel="stylesheet" type="text/css"
    href="inline.css"/>
</head>
<body>
<p id="p1">This is a block of text <span id="s1">This is
another block of text</span> that has another block of
text nested inside.</p>
</body>
</html>
```

Electing not to display content

The stylesheet **display** rule allows content within a XHTML document to be completely ignored by the browser when it specifies a definition of **none**.

This is a very useful feature that allows a single web page to contain content that is customized for desktop browsers and other content that is customized for handheld browsers. The XHTML document can link stylesheets for each type of media. These can simply include a **display:none** rule for content that is not appropriate for that type of browser.

It is important to note that the content that is not displayed is not just hidden – no space on the web page is allocated to that content.

The following example demonstrates how a single XHTML document can be viewed on two different types of browser and present content appropriate to their capabilities in each case.

The **<head>** section of the document contains two **<link>** elements to nominate stylesheets for each type of media. The document's **<body>** contains two **<div>** elements with unique **id** names. Each **<div>** element contains a unique **<img>** element and some text.

The stylesheet for **screen** media elects not to display the contents of the **<div>** element that is intended only for **handheld** media. Similarly, the stylesheet for **handheld** media elects not to display the **<div>** element that is intended only for desktop **screen** media.

Note that the image displayed in the Nokia browser is a smaller version of that displayed in the desktop browser – it is not the same image file resized by **height** and **width** attributes.

The ability to resize images may not be consistent in all browsers. It is more efficient to provide a smaller image file than to download a larger file for the browser to reduce in size – the file size of the small image in this example is only one sixth the size of its larger version.

desktop.css

```
#handheld-content { display: none }

#desktop-content { background-color: silver;
                   color: black }
```

mobile.css

```
#handheld-content { background-color:black;
                    color: white }

#desktop-content { display: none }
```

custom-display.html

Handheld browsers run on devices with limited memory capabilities – consider the files' download size when creating web pages for this type of browser.

```html
<html>
<head>
   <title>Select Display</title>

   <link rel="stylesheet" type="text/css"
     media="screen" href="desktop.css"/>

   <link rel="stylesheet" type="text/css"
     media="handheld" href="mobile.css"/>

</head>
<body>

<div id="desktop-content"><img src="images/lambo-l.gif"
alt="Lamborghini"/><br/>This content is viewable only by
desktop browsers</div>

<div id="handheld-content"><img src="images/lambo-s.gif"
alt="Lamborghini"/>This content is viewable only by
handheld browsers</div>

</body>
</html>
```

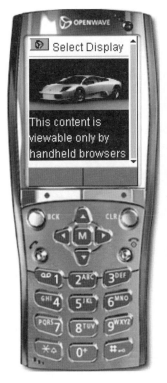

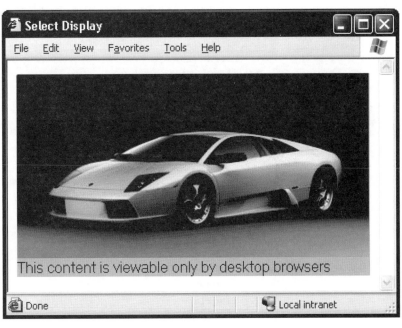

Wrapping text around images

Setting a stylesheet **float** rule allows text to be wrapped around images in a web page. This rule can specify that the image should float to the **left** or **right** of surrounding text. An image floated to the **left** allows text to be wrapped to its **right**, and vice versa.

A **float rule** can also specify **none** if text is explicitly not to be wrapped around the image.

The following example creates classes for each type of **float** rule in the stylesheet on the opposite page. These are assigned to **class** attributes within the **<img>** elements that appear in this XHTML document. The screenshots on the opposite page illustrate how each stylesheet **float** rule affects the content display.

float.html

*The **float:none** style rule mimics the normal default state of desktop browsers.*

```
<html>
<head>
  <title>XHTML Float Position</title>
  <link rel="stylesheet" type="text/css"
    href="float.css"/>
</head>
<body>
<p>The text in this paragraph is interrupted by an image
of this little guy.<img class="no-float" src="images/
lilguy.gif" alt="LilGuy"/> There is no attempt to wrap
this text around the image - it starts right after the
inline image.</p>
<p>The text <img class="float-left" src="images/
lilguy.gif" alt="LilGuy"/>in this paragraph wraps around
the floating box on the left. After the floating box the
lines start at their usual position - this is usually the
left edge of the display area followed by the browser's
page margin.</p>
<p>The text <img class="float-right" src="images/
lilguy.gif" alt="LilGuy"/> in this paragraph wraps around
the floating box on the right. After the floating box the
lines start at their usual position - this is usually the
left edge of the display area followed by the browser's
page margin.</p>
</body>
</html>
```

float.css

```
.no-float     { float: none }

.float-left   { float: left }

.float-right  { float: right }
```

Also see the example on page 154 that adds further control for wrapping text around images.

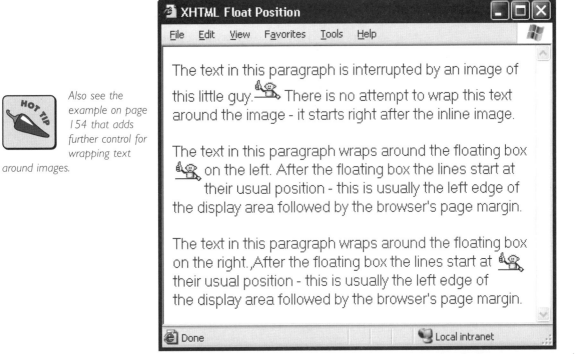

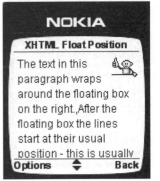

Hiding content

A stylesheet **visibility** rule can be used to make elements of a page invisible by specifying that they should be **hidden**.

It is important to note that an element that is **hidden** by a **visibility:hidden** rule is still treated as a page resource – a blank space is reserved on the page equivalent to the space and position that it would occupy if it were visible. This is the great distinction between using a **visibility:hidden** rule and a **display:none** as no space is reserved on the page with a **display:none** rule.

The XHTML document listed below uses the stylesheet at the top of the opposite page to float an image and wrap text around it:

vis-gfx.html

```
<html>
<head>
  <title>XHTML Visibility</title>
  <link rel="stylesheet" type="text/css"
    href="vis-gfx.css"/>
</head>
<body>
<h3>Today's Weather</h3>  <h4>London</h4>
<p><img class="float-left" src="images/sunny.gif"
alt="sunny face"/>Sunny<br/>High 18&deg;C<br/>Low
15&deg;C</p>
</body>
</html>
```

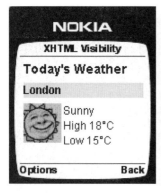

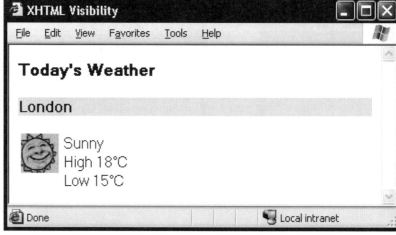

...cont'd

vis-gfx.css

```
h3 { color: red }
h4 { display: block; background-color: yellow }

.float-left { float : left }
```

The **href** attribute in the **<link>** element listed on the opposite page can be modified to use a different stylesheet that includes a **visibility:hidden** rule for the **<img>** element. The modified XHTML file is saved as **vis-txt.html** and uses this new stylesheet:

vis-txt.css

```
h3 { color: red }
h4 { display: block; background-color: yellow }}
.float-left { float : left }

img { visibility: hidden }
```

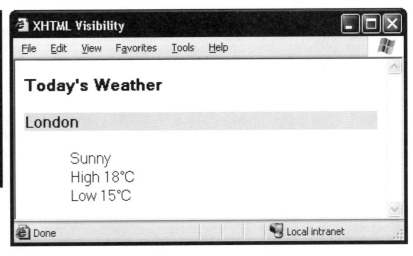

In the screenshots above the text continues to wrap around the space reserved for the invisible image.

Mostly the **visibility** rule is useful in dynamic scripts that can make the image visible by applying a **visible** value to the element's **visibility** property. When a page event occurs a script function is called to apply the new value – this is the same as specifying a **visibility:visible** rule in a stylesheet. Small-device browsers that do not support scripting have little use for the visibility rule.

Disallow wrapping

Text can explicitly be prevented from wrapping around a floated image by setting a stylesheet **clear** rule. This can specify that **left**, **right**, **both** or **none** of its sides should allow a floated image.

The stylesheet in the example below creates a class to **float** images to the **left** of text and another class to keep the **left** side of text **clear** of floated images. The example works as expected in the desktop browser but this handheld browser appears to ignore the **clear** rule.

clear.css

```
.float-left { float: left }

.clear-left { clear: left }
```

clear.html

The clear:both style rule mimics the normal default state of desktop browsers.

```
<html>
<head>
  <title>XHTML Clear Side</title>
  <link rel="stylesheet" type="text/css"
    href="clear.css"/>
</head>
<body>
<p>This text wraps <img class="float-left" src="images/
wine.gif" alt="Wine Image"/>around the wine bottle-and-
glass image on the left.<span class="clear-left">This
text should not wrap.</span> </p>
</body>
</html>
```

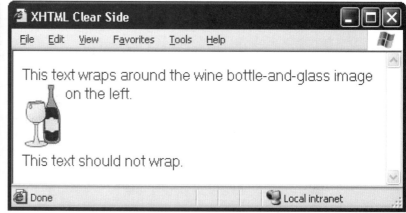

Stylish text

This chapter explores the presentation of text content in XHTML documents. There are examples illustrating how to influence the manner of textual display with stylesheet rules.

Covers

Font families | 156

Font size | 157

Font style & weight | 158

Font shorthand | 160

Text & content alignment | 161

Text decoration | 162

Indenting text | 163

Spacing text | 164

Line height | 165

Text capitalization | 166

Chapter Thirteen

Font families

A stylesheet **font-family** rule suggests a generic font to be used by the browser. Valid generic **font-family** names are **serif**, **sans-serif**, **cursive**, **monospace** and **fantasy**. The **font-family** rule can also suggest several specific fonts as a comma-delimited list. Both **cursive** and **fantasy font-family** styles are more decorative than the other plainer fonts used in this example:

font-family.css

```
#s1{ font-family: serif }
#s2 { font-family: sans-serif }
#s3 {font-family: monospace }
#s4 { font-family: cursive }
#s5 { font-family: fantasy }
#s6 { font-family: impact,modern,cursive }
```

font-family.html

```
<html>
<head>
   <title>XHTML Font-Family</title>
   <link rel="stylesheet" type="text/css"
     href="font-family.css"/>
</head>
<body><p>
<span id="s1">Serif</span>
<span id="s2">Sans-Serif</span>
<span id="s3">Monospace</span>  <br/>
<span id="s4">Cursive</span>
<span id="s5">Fantasy</span>  <br/>
<span id="s6">Impact,Modern or Generic Cursive</span>
</p></body>
</html>
```

A *font-family* rule overcomes the difficulty that not all systems have the same fonts installed – so the browser can select the most appropriate installed font for the suggested family.

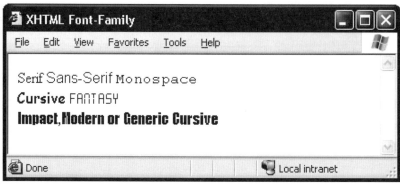

Font size

The size of font can be suggested by a stylesheet **font-size** rule. This can specify an exact size as a point size, with the suffix **pt,** or as a relative size to the current font stated as a **%** percentage, or with the terms **larger** or **smaller**.

The following example first sets a general font size of **12pt** for the entire paragraph then adds rules to suggest a greater specific size and some relative sizes. Note that small-device browsers may not implement specific font sizes due to their limited display areas.

font-size.css

```css
p { font-size: 12pt }
#f-20 { font-size: 20pt }
#smaller { font-size: 70% }
#bigger { font-size: larger }
```

font-size.html

```html
<html>
<head>
   <title>Font-Size</title>
   <link rel="stylesheet" type="text/css"
     href="font-size.css"/>
</head>
<body><p>
This is a 12-point font size.<br/>
<span id="f-20">and this is a 20-point font size.</span>
<br/>SIZE CAN BE <span id="smaller">REDUCED</span>
OR <span id="bigger">ENLARGED</span>
</p></body>
</html>
```

Set specific font sizes to override the browser's text size options.

Font style & weight

The appearance of text can be specified with a stylesheet **font-style** rule to select upright or slanting characters. The default **font-style** is to use upright characters, but setting the **font-style** to **italic** will normally display text with slanting characters.

A **font-style** of **oblique** will also generally display as italics.

If the text generally uses italics a **font-style** of **normal** can be used to explicitly specify that the text should have upright characters. Both **italic** and **normal font-style** is illustrated in this example:

font-style.css

```
#s1 { font-style: italic }
#p2 { font-style: italic }
#s2 { font-style: normal }
```

font-style.html

```
<html>
<head>
  <title>XHTML Font-Style</title>
  <link rel="stylesheet" type="text/css"
    href="font-style.css"/>
</head>
<body>
<p id="p1">This paragraph uses default styling but
<span id="s1">italic style</span> can be applied.</p>
<p id="p2">This paragraph uses italic styling but
<span id="s2">normal styling</span> can be applied.</p>
</body>
</html>
```

*An **oblique** font-style may electronically generate an **italic** font by slanting a default upright font.*

The preferred boldness of text can be suggested with a stylesheet **font-weight** rule. Simply specifying a **bold font-weight** will display the text in a bold font.

Alternatively, the **font-weight** can be specified numerically in a range from 100 to 900 – where 100 is the lightest font and 900 is the boldest font. Normally-weighted text is around 500.

This example sets a piece of **bold** text then demonstrates the effect of adding **font-weight** from normal weight to the boldest:

font-weight.css

```
.bold { font-weight: bold }
.f-500 { font-weight: 500 }
.f-700 { font-weight: 700 }
.f-900 { font-weight: 900 }
```

font-weight.html

```
<html>
<head>
  <title>XHTML Font-Weight</title>
  <link rel="stylesheet" type="text/css"
    href="font-weight.css"/>
</head>
<body>
<p>Here is some <span class="bold">bold</span> text.<br/>
<span class="f-500"> 500 </span>
<span class="f-700"> 700 </span>
<span class="f-900"> 900 </span> </p>
</body>
</html>
```

Setting a lighter *font-weight* below 500 seldom changes the appearance.

Font shorthand

The font properties for **family**, **style**, **size** and **weight** can be specified by a single stylesheet **font** rule with this syntax:

```
font { font-style font-weight font-size font-family }
```

Any of the font properties can be omitted from this list but if they are included they should appear in this order.

The example below uses the shorthand **font** rule to specify various font settings for a tag, an id and a class:

font.css

```
p { font: 12pt serif }
#s1 { font: bold 28pt }
.doric { font: italic bold 16pt }
```

font.html

```
<html>
<head>
   <title>XHTML Font</title>
   <link rel="stylesheet" type="text/css"
     href="font.css"/>
</head>
<body>
<p>The main attraction of Gortys is the<br/>
<span id="s1">Code of Laws</span><br/>
These were carved on massive blocks of stone by the
<span class="doric">Dorians</span> </p>
</body>
</html>
```

*Specific named fonts must still be set with a **font-family** rule.*

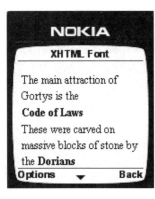

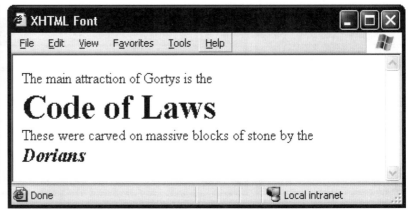

Text & content alignment

All types of content can be aligned within its content box, or containing element, by a stylesheet **text-align** rule. The rule can specify whether the alignment should be **left**, **right** or **center**.

This example aligns text in three **<div>** content boxes and demonstrates a centered image:

alignment.css

```
div { border: 1px solid silver;
      padding: 5px; margin: 5px }
#d1 { text-align: left }
#d2 { text-align: right }
#d3 { text-align: center }
```

alignment.html

```
<html>
<head>
   <title>XHTML Alignment</title>
   <link rel="stylesheet" type="text/css"
      href="alignment.css"/>
</head>
<body>
<div id="d1">text-align is left</div>
<div id="d2">text-align is right</div>
<div id="d3">text-align is center<br/>
<img src="lilguy.gif" alt="LilGuy"/></div>
</body>
</html>
```

The rule *text-align:center* replaces the old HTML **<center>** element.

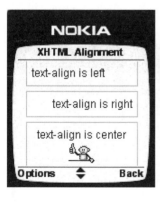

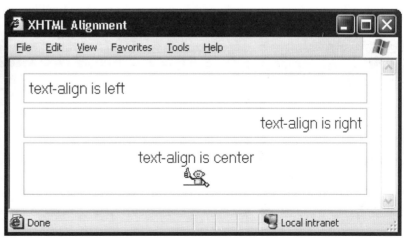

Text decoration

A stylesheet **text-decoration** rule can suggest additional features to **underline** text or to specify that the text should **blink** on and off. Alternatively it may specify **none** to explicitly indicate that no text features should be added.

Beware of using **blink** rules frequently as flashing text can be very irritating. Internet Explorer does not support the **blink** rule because of this reason.

This example demonstrates underlined text and blinking text in the Nokia and Mozilla browsers:

decor.css

```
div { border: 1px solid silver;
      padding: 5px; margin: 5px }
#d1 { text-decoration: underline }
#d2 { text-decoration: blink }
```

decor.html

A *text-decoration underline* rule replaces the old HTML *<u>* element.

```
<html>
<head>
  <title>XHTML Text Decor</title>
  <link rel="stylesheet" type="text/css"
    href="decor.css"/>
</head>
<body>
<div id="d1">This is underlined text.</div>
<div id="d2">This text may blink.</div>
</body>
</html>
```

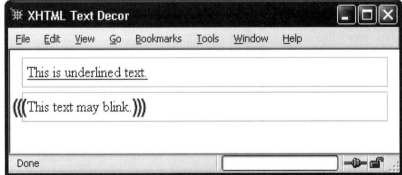

Indenting text

A stylesheet **text-indent** rule can suggest that the browser should indent text by a specified distance. This can either be expressed as a fixed distance, such as a number of **px** pixels, or as a **%** percentage of the total width of the display area.

Small-device browsers may not support the **text-indent** rule due to the restricted size of their displays.

In the following example a **text-indent** rule suggests that the beginning of each paragraph should be indented by 10% of the overall width of the browser's display area:

indentation.css

```
p { text-indent: 10% }
```

indentation.html

```
<html>
<head>
   <title>Text Indent</title>
   <link rel="stylesheet"  type="text/css"
   href="indentation.css"/>
</head>
<body>
<p>One of the best adventures on Crete is to walk
through the Gorge of Samaria.</p>
<p>It is the longest gorge in Europe.</p>
</body>
</html>
```

Spacing text

Normally the browser determines how text should be spaced but stylesheet **letter-spacing** and **word-spacing** rules can suggest alternatives to the default spacing.

Both **letter-spacing** and **word-spacing** rules can specify additional spacing to the default spacing either as a fixed **px** pixel distance, or as a **%** percentage of the overall display width, or as an **em** relative size to the character's font.

The example below adds three extra pixels to the spacing between all letters in a paragraph plus twenty extra pixels between the words in a **<span>** element. These rules are ignored by both the Nokia browser and the Openwave browser.

space.css

```
p { letter-spacing: 3px }

span { word-spacing: 20px }
```

space.html

*Use **em** units in preference to **px** pixels to display text spacing more appropriate to the text's font size.*

```
<html>
<head>
   <title>XHTML Spacing</title>
   <link rel="stylesheet" type="text/css"
     href="space.css"/>
</head>
<body>
<p>Crete, a tangerine-growing country, also produces
<span>a delicious liquer called mandarini.</span></p>
</body>
</html>
```

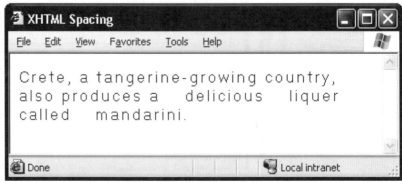

Line height

A stylesheet **line-height** rule can suggest an amount of additional spacing to be added between each line of text.

This can be specified as a fixed **px** pixel distance or as a **%** percentage of the current font size. For instance, with a **font-size** of 12pt setting a **line-height** rule at 300% would create additional line spacing of 36pt.

In the example below the general font-size is 12pt but the **line-height** rule adds another 36pt spacing over all text.

lines.css

```
p { font-size: 12pt; line-height: 300% }

span { font-size: 36pt }
```

lines.html

```
<html>
<head>
   <title>Line Height</title>
   <link rel="stylesheet" type="text/css"
     href="lines.css"/>
</head>
<body>
<p>General font size in this paragragh is 12pt.<br/>
But here is some<span>36pt</span> text.<br/>
All line heights are also 36pt.</p>
</body>
</html>
```

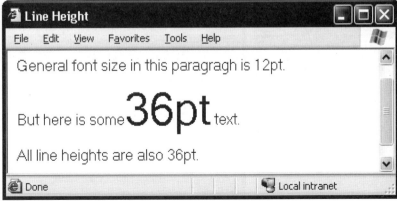

Text capitalization

The stylesheet **text-transform** rule can be useful to convert the capitalization of text. It may be used to transform text into **uppercase** or **lowercase**, and it can make the first letter of each word into a capital letter when it is set to **capitalize**.

In the following example text contained in three **<div>** elements is transformed by the browser to illustrate each of the three **text-transform** possibilities:

transform.css

```
div { border: 1px solid silver;
      padding: 5px; margin: 5px }
#d1 { text-transform: uppercase }
#d2 { text-transform: lowercase }
#d3 { text-transform: capitalize }
```

transform.html

Note that **text-transform** rules only work with standard Latin characters.

```
<html>
<head>
  <title>XHTML Text Transform</title>
  <link rel="stylesheet" type="text/css"
    href="transform.css"/>
</head>
<body>
  <div id="d1">now uppercase</div>
  <div id="d2">NOW LOWERCASE</div>
  <div id="d3">now capitalized</div>
</body>
</html>
```

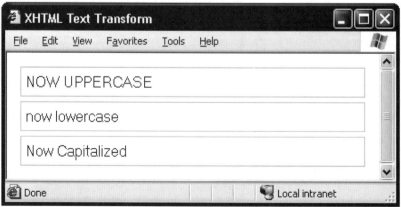

Controlling backgrounds

This chapter demonstrates how stylesheet rules can control how background images of a XHTML document are displayed in a browser. Examples also illustrate different page formats and graphical pointers for those browsers that display cursors.

Covers

Background image | 168

Repeating background image | 170

Positioning background image | 171

Fixing background image | 172

Background shorthand | 173

Page formats | 174

Cursors | 176

Chapter Fourteen

Background image

As alternative to specifying a colored background with a **background-color** rule, an image can be used as its background. The stylesheet **background-image** rule states the location of the image as an absolute or relative address. This must be contained within a pair of quotes and is defined between plain brackets following the term **url**.

Browsers normally 'tile' the image, both horizontally and vertically, across the entire background.

This example tiles a partly-transparent GIF **background-image** over a specified **background-color** in the desktop browser but the Nokia browser ignores this **background-image** rule:

bg-img.css

```
body { background-color: aqua;
        background-image:url("images/mug.gif") }
```

bg-img.html

```
<html>
<head>
  <title>Back Image</title>
  <link rel="stylesheet" type="text/css"
    href="bg-img.css"/>
</head>
<body>
<h1>Coffee Time!</h1>
</body>
</html>
```

Refer back to page 50 for more on **color** *and* **background-color** *stylesheet rules.*

There are many XHTML elements to which a **background-image** rule can be applied – each can specify a background image for that particular element. Most frequently **background-image** rules are used to specify a background image for **<body>**, **<div>**, **<table>** or **<td>** elements.

To demonstrate individual **background-image** rules the following example applies separate background images for two **<div>** elements within a single XHTML document:

div-bg.css

```
body { background-color: white }
div { width: 100%; height: 35px; margin-top: 10px;
      border: 1px solid black; background-color: silver }
#d1 { background-image: url("images/mug.gif") }
#d2 { background-image: url("images/box.gif") }
```

div-bg.html

This example is repeating these single images

– the dark areas in the mug image are transparent.

```
<html>
<head>
  <title>Back Image</title>
  <link rel="stylesheet" type="text/css"
    href="div-bg.css"/>
</head>
<body>

  <div id="d1">Division 1</div>
  <div id="d2">Division 2</div>

</body>
</html>
```

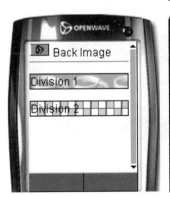

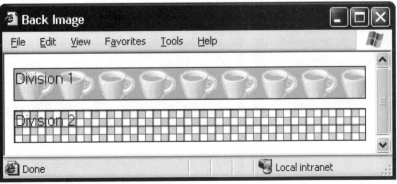

Repeating background image

The stylesheet **background-repeat** rule can specify whether a background image should be tiled horizontally or vertically. Setting this rule to **repeat-x** tiles the image horizontally and **repeat-y** tiles the image vertically.

The example below uses stylesheet **background-repeat** rules to control how a background image is tiled in two table cells:

bg-repeat.css

```
body { text-align: center } table { width: 100% }
td { background-color: black; color: white;
     font-weight: bold;
     background-image: url("images/box.gif") }
#cell-1 { background-repeat: repeat-y }
#cell-2 { background-repeat: repeat-x;
            text-indent: 20px }
```

bg-repeat.html

```
<html>
<head>
  <title>Back Repeat</title>
  <link rel="stylesheet" type="text/css"
    href="bg-repeat.css" />
</head>
<body>
<table summary="Simple Table"> <tr>
  <td id="cell-1"><br/>repeat-y</td>
  <td id="cell-2">repeat-x</td> </tr>
</table>
</body>
</html>
```

The Nokia mobile browser does not support the **background-image** *rule.*

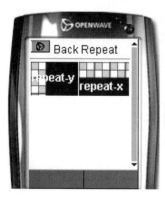

Positioning background image

The position of a background image can be specified with a stylesheet **background-position** rule expressed in **px** pixels, or **%** percentages, or as **top**, **bottom**, **left**, **right** or **center**. If only one value is specified it sets the horizontal position – but if two values are specified the second also sets the vertical position. This example centers a background image in the first table cell and sets the second image centrally at the bottom of the next cell.

bg-position.css

```
body { text-align: center } table { width: 100% }
td { background-color: silver; height: 50px;
     border: 1px solid black;
       background-image: url("images/box.gif");
       background-repeat: no-repeat }
#cell-1 { background-position: center }
#cell-2 { background-position: 50% 100% }
```

bg-position.html

```
<html>
<head>
   <title>Back Position</title>
   <link rel="stylesheet" type="text/css"
    href="bg-position.css" />
</head>
<body>
<table summary="Simple Table"> <tr>
   <td id="cell-1">Center</td>
   <td id="cell-2">50% 100%</td> </tr>
</table>
</body>
</html>
```

*Note that the **background-repeat** rule in this example specifies **no-repeat** to stop the browser tiling the image.*

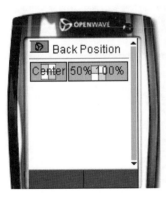

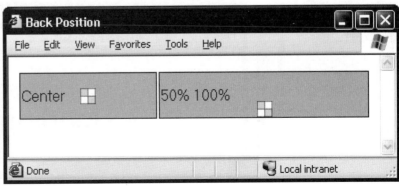

Fixing background image

Typically background images will scroll along with the document content but the position of a background image can be **fixed** by a stylesheet **background-attachment** rule. This enables the position of the image to remain constant even when the page is scrolled.

In the example below stylesheet rules control the position of a background image, the direction in which it should be tiled, and permanently fix it to that position in the browser window:

bg-fixed.css

```
body { background-attachment: fixed; text-align: center;
       background-position: 0% 35px;
       background-repeat: repeat-x;
       background-image: url("images/box.gif") }
```

bg-fixed.html

```
<html>
<head>
  <title>Back Fixed</title>
  <link rel="stylesheet" type="text/css"
    href="bg-fixed.css" />
</head>
  <body> <p> <br/> <br/> </p> <h1>Heading</h1> </body>
</html>
```

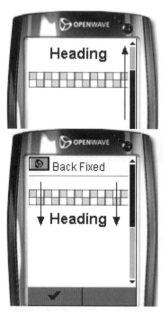

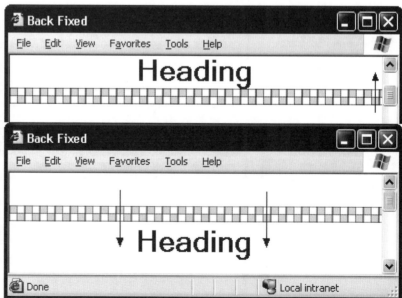

Background shorthand

All the background properties of an element can be specified together with a shorthand **background** rule. This can set some or all of the background's color, image, repeat, position and attachment properties – listed in any order.

A single **background** rule is meant to replace separate rules for each individual background property but may not always be desirable.

In the following example a **background** rule sets a background color, image and repeat instruction. These could have been specified individually with separate **background-color**, **background-image** and **background-repeat** rules to clarify their purpose in the stylesheet.

background.css

```
body { background: silver url("images/gift.gif")
       repeat-x }
div { width: 100%; margin-top: 70px;
      border: 1px solid black; text-align: center }
```

background.html

```
<html>
<head>
   <title>Background</title>
   <link rel="stylesheet" type="text/css"
     href="background.css"/>
</head>
<body>
<div id="d1">Gift Ideas</div>
</body>
</html>
```

Page formats

When designing web pages that are intended for both desktop and mobile browsers it is best to begin by considering how the page will appear in the mobile browser. It is easier to extend a mobile-oriented web page for a desktop browser than the other way round.

If a desktop-oriented web page is the starting point it is best to consider each of its components. Only the core components should be used when developing the mobile-oriented web page. For instance, a traditional web page describing a small selection of books might include the title, a synopsis and an image of the cover for each one of the books. A mobile-oriented version of this page could just list each one of the titles as a hyperlink to its synopsis. Each synopsis page might also include a hyperlink to the image of that book's cover. This allows the user to selectively view all the information available in the traditional page, but in a more compact manner.

It is also worth noting that the format of desktop browsers is usually landscape (wider than high) – whereas the format of mobile browsers is usually portrait (higher than wide). Good page design should provide content in the appropriate format.

*Do not use a **visibility** rule to hide the inappropriate table as the browser still reserves space for that **hidden table** in the page – refer back to page 153.*

The XHTML example on the opposite page links the two stylesheets listed below to display a table of ten cells in a format appropriate to the media type. The table has three rows and four columns on desktop browsers but five rows and two columns on mobile browsers. A stylesheet **display** rule instructs each browser to ignore the inappropriate table.

format-landscape.css

```
#portrait-table{ display: none }

table { width: 100%; font-weight: bold }
th { background-color: red; color: white }
td { background-color: yellow; padding: 3px;
     border: 1px solid black }
```

format-portrait.css

```
#landscape-table{ display: none }

table { width: 100%; font-weight: bold }
th { background-color: red; color: white }
td { background-color: yellow; padding: 1px;
     border: 1px solid black }
```

...cont'd

format.html

The table in this example lists some other topics of the books in this series – each topic could easily be made into a hyperlink to a synopsis page containing a further hyperlink to that book's cover image.

```html
<html>
<head> <title>Page Format</title>

  <link rel="stylesheet" type="text/css"
    media="screen" href="format-landscape.css"/>

  <link rel="stylesheet" type="text/css"
    media="handheld" href="format-portrait.css"/>

</head>
<body>

<table id="landscape-table" summary="Easy Steps Table">
<tr> <th colspan="4">in easy steps</th> </tr>
<tr> <td>PERL</td> <td>HTML</td> <td>C</td> <td>C++</td>
</tr>
<tr> <td>Java</td> <td>XML</td> <td>JSP</td> <td>SQL</td> </tr>
</table>

<table id="portrait-table" summary="Easy Steps Table">
<tr> <th colspan="2">in easy steps</th> </tr>
<tr> <td>Java</td> <td>XML</td>     </tr>
<tr> <td>JSP</td>   <td>C</td> </tr>
<tr> <td>SQL</td>   <td>HTML</td>     </tr>
<tr> <td>C++</td>   <td>PERL</td>     </tr>
</table>

</body>
</html>
```

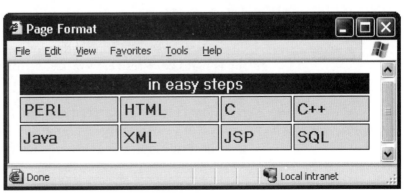

Cursors

In browsers that display floating on-screen cursors, the type of pointer to be displayed when the user moves the cursor over elements can be set with a stylesheet **cursor** rule.

Common valid pointer values include the **default**, **crosshair**, **move**, **text**, **wait**, and **help** pointers that are described in this table:

Name	Cursor	Pointer Type
default	▵	Browser's default cursor
pointer	☝	Hand pointer indicating a link
crosshair	+	Pinpoint selector
move	✥	Selection relocator
text	I	Text highlighter
wait	⧗	Program busy indicator
help	▵?	Help available indicator
resize	⇒	Edge indicator
url	⊘	Specify remote cursor address

The **resize** cursor is a pointer that indicates a direction and can be set as **n-resize**, **s-resize**, **w-resize**, **e-resize**, **ne-resize**, **nw-resize**, **se-resize**, or **sw-resize**. The table above shows the **e-resize** cursor.

A custom cursor can be specified with a **cursor** rule stating the location of a cursor image with the term **url**. For instance, this stylesheet rule indicates a custom cursor to be used:

```
cursor: url( "http://domain/folder/special.cur" );
```

XHTML Mobile Profile

This chapter introduces the XHTML Mobile Profile specification which provides support for some features that are not available in the XHTML Basic specification. There are examples that demonstrate each additional feature.

Covers

What is XHTML Mobile Profile ? | 178

List attributes | 179

Style support | 180

Presentation elements | 182

Grouping elements | 184

What's next ? | 186

Chapter Fifteen

What is XHTML Mobile Profile ?

When the World Wide Web Consortium (W3C) introduced XHTML Basic the Japanese telecommunications giant NTT DoCoMo was already using a subset of HTML called Compact HTML (cHTML) for its i-Mode cellphone system. As Western cellphone manufacturers, such as Nokia and Ericsson, adopted XHTML Basic as their preferred language an undesirable two-tier situation arose.

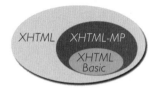

In order to resolve this issue NTT DoCoMo approached the WAP Forum (now the Open Mobile Alliance) with a view to creating a single universally acceptable solution. The result is the XHTML Mobile Profile specification.

XHTML Mobile Profile is a superset of XHTML Basic – it includes all the features of XHTML Basic plus some additional features from the full XHTML 1.0 specification. So XHTML Mobile Profile is a subset of XHTML but with more features than XHTML Basic. These additional features replicate some of the popular features in cHTML.

XHTML Mobile Profile Document Headers

Like all XHTML documents a XHTML Mobile Profile document should begin with a XML declaration stating the version number. This must be followed by a **<!DOCTYPE>** tag containing the name and location of the special XHTML Mobile Profile DTD.

```
<?xml version="1.0" ?>

<!DOCTYPE html PUBLIC
   "-//WAPFORUM//DTD XHTML Mobile 1.0//EN"
   "http://www.wapforum.org/DTD/xhtml-mobile10.dtd" >
```

The XML and DTD declarations listed above begin each of the examples in this chapter but these have been omitted from the listed code to save space. Please remember that they must be inserted before the listed code to create valid documents.

XHTML Mobile Profile documents can be validated online by the W3C's Markup Validation Service described on page 12 – although it may not offer a verification image for this specification.

List attributes

Ordered lists start numbering each list item from 1 by default but XHTML Mobile Profile allows a **start** attribute to be added to the **<ol>** tag to specify a different number to start from.

Similarly, the XHTML Mobile Profile specification also provides a **value** attribute for the **<li>** tag to specify what an item should be numbered.

List items are numbered incremental to the number allocated to the previous list item – by whatever method.

The ordered list in the document below is instructed to **start** numbering from seven. Its third item is given a list **value** of ten so its fourth item automatically becomes number eleven:

mp-lists.html

```
<html>
<head>
   <title>Lists</title>
</head>
<body>

  <ol start="7">
    <li >Orange</li>
    <li >Apple</li>
    <li value="10">Pear</li>
    <li>Peach</li>
  </ol>

</body>
</html>
```

Style support

Probably the most important advantage of the XHTML Mobile Profile specification is its ability to add stylesheet rules to a document without a separate stylesheet file.

This allows a **\<style\>** element to be incorporated within the document's **\<head\>** section. Stylesheet rules can then be listed between its **\<style\>** and **\</style\>** tags in the normal way – as demonstrated by the following example:

mp-style.html

```
<html>
<head>
   <title>Style</title>

   <style type="text/css">
     h1 { color: blue; font-style: italic }
     #d1 { border: 5px dashed red; padding: 5px }
     .rev { background-color: black; color: white;
       padding: 5px; margin-top: 5px; font-weight: bold }
   </style>

</head>
<body>
<h1>Added Style</h1>
<div id="d1">Division 1</div>
<div class="rev">Division 2</div>
</body>
</html>
```

*Remember to include a **type** attribute inside a **\<style\>** tag.*

In addition to providing a **<style>** element the XHTML Mobile Profile specification also allows a **style** attribute to be added to most elements. This means that style rules can be specified for text 'inline' – without the need for a separate stylesheet.

Although this would seem to be an advantage the use of the inline **style** attribute is to be discouraged. Imagine a document with lots of inline styles, then consider how much more difficult it is to change those rules compared to the ease with a separate stylesheet.

The short example below demonstrates how the inline **style** attribute can quickly complicate content code:

mp-inline-style.html

```
<html>
<head>
   <title>Style</title>
</head>
<body  style="background-color:yellow">

<h1  style="color:blue;text-decoration:underline">
Greek Drinks</h1>

<p>Anise-flavoured <img src="lilguy.gif" alt="LilGuy"/>
<span  style="background-color:red;color:white;font-
weight:bold">o&uacute;zo</span> is a refreshing <span
style="color:green;font-weight:900">aperitif</span>.
</p>
</body>
</html>
```

Adding style inline makes the code harder to read and more difficult to maintain – it's better to have a separate stylesheet.

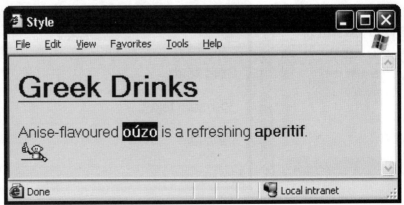

Presentation elements

The XHTML Mobile Profile specification provides a few presentational elements that enable text to be styled without the need for dedicated style rules.

The **<b>** element instructs the browser to display any text between its **<b>** and **</b>** tags in a bolder font.

Similarly, the **<i>** element instructs the browser to display any text between its **<i>** and **</i>** tags in an italicized font.

The empty **<hr>** element cannot be replicated by a stylesheet rule and must always end with a final **/** character. It instructs the browser to draw a horizontally ruled line within the limits of its content box – in the example below this is the document body:

mp-rule-bold-italic.html

The **<hr>** element can only draw lines between blocks of content – it cannot be used inline within text.

```
<html>
<head>
   <title>Presentation</title>
</head>
<body>

<div> <b>Bold text</b> </div>
<hr/>
<div>Standard  text</div>
<hr/>
<div> <i>Italic text</i> </div>

</body>
</html>
```

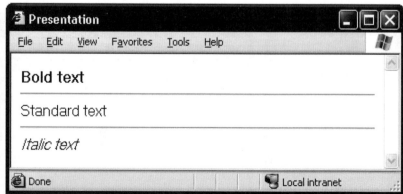

Text can easily be enhanced with the XHTML Mobile Profile **<big>** element which promotes the current font to a more prominent appearance. Text within **<big>** and **</big>** tags may appear in a larger font size or as a bolder font.

Conversely, text can be made less prominent by using a XHTML Mobile Profile **<small>** element. Text that is enclosed between **<small>** and **</small>** tags may appear as a smaller font size or be reduced from a bold font to a normal font weight.

The example below illustrates how different browsers might apply these elements. In the desktop browser the **<big>** element promotes the text to a bolder font, whereas the same element in the mobile browser promotes the text to a larger font size.

mp-big-small.html

```
<html>
<head>
   <title>Presentation</title>
</head>
<body>

<div> <big>Big text</big> </div>
<hr/>
<div>Standard  text</div>
<hr/>
<div> <small>Small  text</small> </div>

</body>
/html>
```

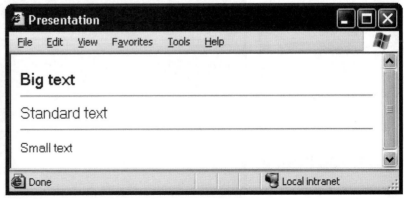

Grouping elements

The XHTML Mobile Profile provides a **\<fieldset\>** element that can be used to group together a number of related elements between **\<fieldset\>** and **\</fieldset\>** tags. Typically it is used to group together a number of related form elements. A style applied to a **\<fieldset\>** element is also applied to its grouped elements.

The example below applies an inline **background-color** rule to a **\<fieldset\>** – which is applied to its grouped radio input elements:

mp-fieldset.html

Many browsers indicate a
\<fieldset\>
graphically –
usually by
drawing a box enclosing all the grouped elements.

```
<html>
<head>
   <title>Fieldset</title>
</head>
<body>
<form action="parser.cgi" method="post">

<fieldset style="background-color: orange">
   Fizzy drinks:<br/>
   <input type="radio" name="pop" value="lemonade"/>
   Lemonade <br/>
   <input type="radio" name="pop" value="cola"/>Cola <br/>
   <input type="radio" name="pop" value="orange"/>Orange
</fieldset>

<p> <input type="submit" value="Submit"/> </p>
</form>
</body>
</html>
```

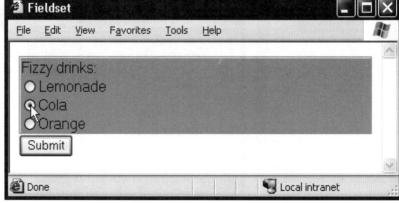

...cont'd

Related **<option>** elements in a **<select>** element can also be grouped together with a **<optgroup>** element. The grouped elements are contained between **<optgroup>** and **</optgroup>** tags. This example uses the **<optgroup>** element's **label** attribute to specify a label for each group of elements:

mp-optgroup.html

*Note that different browsers display **<option>** lists in a variety of styles. It is best to let the browser choose how these should be displayed – be wary of setting custom style rules which the browser may override.*

```
<html>
<head>
   <title>Optgroup</title>
</head>
<body>
<form action="parser.cgi" method="post">
<p>
<select name="breakfast">
   <optgroup label="With Toast...">
     <option value="jam">Strawberry Jam</option>
     <option value="mar">Orange Marmalade</option>
   </optgroup>
   <optgroup label="Cereal...">
     <option value="cor">Corn Flakes</option>
     <option value="ric">Rice Krispies</option>
   </optgroup> <input type="submit" value="Submit"/>
</p>
</form>
</body>
</html>
```

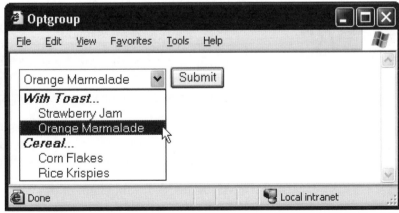

What's next ?

Communication service companies around the world are introducing third-generation (3G) capability for wireless devices which vastly increases bandwidth. This enables small handheld devices to receive large data packets without the latency problem inherent in previous technology.

Wireless access to 3G services are facilitated by the increasing number of hotspots providing support for Wi-Fi – the 802.11 standard for wireless connectivity.

This combination of increased bandwidth and connectivity introduces a whole host of possibilities for mobile devices, such as streaming video on the move – with XHTML.

Websites written in old HTML code cannot be viewed on mobile devices that insist upon the efficiency of valid XHTML code. Web developers are, however, beginning to understand the significance of enabling their content to be accessible via the burgeoning number of handheld devices. This means they must change their attitude to website design and shift focus from aesthetic appeal to a more data-centered approach – with XHTML.

As mobile devices increase in power and memory capability they will have the capacity to provide client-side logic. Some cellphones are currently supplied with support for the Java 2 Micro Edition that allows them to execute downloaded Java applications. There are moves from Macromedia to build support for Flash animations into mobile devices too. Both Java and Flash applications could be embedded into XHTML web pages.

www.w3c.org

To keep up to date with the latest developments it is a good idea to regularly visit the W3C website. One exciting development currently underway, that could possibly be incorporated into XHTML in the future, is their work on VoiceXML. Web pages may one day talk to you using speech synthesis!

Markup language for the internet has come a long way since a college student named Marc Anderssen added support for an **<img>** tag to the Mosaic web browser back in 1993.

Today Marc is a leading light of the W3C and XHTML is destined to be the language of the internet – happy coding!

Index

Abbreviation element <abbr> 46
   title attribute 46
Absolute address 96
Accesskey attribute 87
Acronym element <acronym> 46
   title attribute 46
Action attribute 118
ActiveX control 104–105
Address element <address> 44
Advisory elements 46
Align attribute 78
Alt attribute 96
Anchor element <a> 86
   accesskey attribute 87
   charset attribute 93
   href attribute 86, 88
   hreflang attribute 93
   rel attribute 94
   rev attribute 94
   tabindex attribute 92
   target attribute 115
   type attribute 93
Applet parameters 103
Attributes 18
Authoring tips 18

Background property
   background rule 173
   background-attachment rule 172
   background-color rule 50, 168
   background-image rule 168
   background-position rule 171
   background-repeat rule 170

Base element <base> 32
   href attribute 32
Bigger text element <big> 183
Blockquote element <blockquote> 41
Body element <body> 17
Bold element <b> 182
Border attribute 114
Border property
   border shorthand rule 138
   border-color rule 135
   border-style rule 135
   border-style-bottom rule 136
   border-style-left rule 136
   border-style-right rule 136
   border-style-top rule 136
   border-width rule 135
Border style 136
   color 73
   solid 73
   width 73
Break element
  36
Bullet point
   circle 63
   decimal 65
   disc 62
   image 66
   lower-alpha 65
   lower-roman 65
   square 64
   upper-alpha 65
   upper-roman 65

Cache control 24
Caption element <caption> 74
Cascading stylesheet
   classes 52
   efficiency 57
   selectors 50
Character entities 38
Character sets 14
Checkboxes 122
Checked attribute 123
Circle bullet 63
Citation element <cite> 47
   title attribute 47
Class property 52
Classid attribute 108

Clear property   154
Clear rule
   left, right, both, none   154
Code element <code>   45
Code validation   12
Codebase attribute   106
Color
   hexadecimal numbers   58
   names   58
Cols attribute   111
Colspan attribute   77
Comments element <!-- -->   18
Common Gateway Interface (CGI)   118
Content attribute   22
Content box   134
   border property   134
   margin property   134
   padding property   134
Core attributes
   class, id, title   52
Cursor property   176

Decimal bullet   65
Definition description element <dd>   67
Definition element <dfn>   47
   title attribute   47
Definition list element <dl>   67
Definition term element <dt>   67
Disc bullet   62
Display property   174
   inline, block   146
   none   148
Division element <div>   34, 148
Doctype declaration   15
Document structure   17
Document Type Definition (DTD)   110
   XHTML Basic   15
   XHTML Frameset   11
   XHTML Mobile Profile   178
   XHTML Strict   11
   XHTML Transitional   11
Dublin Core Metadata Initiative   20

Embedded objects
   Flash movie player   108
   image object   99
   Java applet   102
   QuickTime media player   106
   sound   104
   text object   100
   video   105
   XHTML object   101
Emphasis element <em>   42
Empty tags   18
Enctype attribute   118
Entities   38
Extensible HyperText Markup Language (XHTML)   9

Fieldset element <fieldset>   184
File extension .html   12
Flash movie player   108
Font property
   font shorthand rule   160
   font-family rule   156
   font-size rule   157
   font-style rule   158
   font-weight rule   159
Form element <form>   118
   action attribute   118
   enctype attribute   118
   get method   118
   method attribute   118
   post method   118
Form handler   118
Fragment anchors #   88
Frame element <frame>   111
   frameborder attribute   114
   marginheight attribute   114
   marginwidth attribute   114
   name attribute   115
   noresize attribute   114

scrolling attribute   114
src attribute   111
Frameborder attribute   114
Frameholder document   110
Frameset DTD   110
Frameset element <frameset>   111
  cols attribute   111
  nested frames   113
  rows attribute   112
  wildcard value ★   111

G

Get method, form submission   118

H

Handheld media   28, 148
Head element <head>   17, 20
  profile attribute   20
  xml:lang attribute   20
Heading elements <h1> - <h6>   37
Height attribute   96
Hidden inputs   125
Horizontal rule element <hr>   182
Href attribute   86
HTML element <html>   16
  xml:lang attribute   16
  xmlns attribute   16
Http-equiv attribute   24
Hyperlink   86
HyperText Markup Language (HTML)   8

I

Id property   88
  id attribute   54
Image bullet   66

Image element <img>   90, 96
  alt attribute   90
  class attribute   96
  height attribute   96
  id attribute   96
  longdesc attribute   96
  src attribute   90
  title attribute   90, 96
  width attribute   96
Image links   90
Input element <input>
  checkbox type   122
  checked attribute   123
  hidden type   125
  id attribute   130
  maxlength attribute   120
  name attribute   120
  password type   121
  radio type   124
  reset type   132
  size attribute   120
  submit type   118
  tabindex attribute   123
  text type   120
  type attribute   120
  value attribute   122
Italic element <i>   182

J

Java applet
  java: protocol   102
JavaScript   26

K

Keyboard element <kbd>   48
  title attribute   48

L

Label element <label>   130
  for attribute   130
Language codes   16
Letter-spacing property   164
Line break element
   36
Line-height property   165
Link element <link>   28
  charset attribute   28
  href attribute   28
  hreflang attribute   28
  media attribute   28, 52
  rel attribute   28, 30
  rev attribute   28
  type attribute   28
List
  definition list element <dl>   67
  ordered list element <ol>   60
    start attribute   179
    value attribute   179
  unordered list element <ul>   61
List element <li>   60–61
List-style rule   70
List-style shorthand   70
List-style-image property   66
List-style-position property   68
List-style-type property   62

M

Macromedia Dreamweaver MX   12
Margin property
  margin shorthand rule   143
  margin-bottom rule   142
  margin-left rule   142
  margin-right rule   142
  margin-top rule   142
Marginheight attribute   114
Marginwidth attribute   114
Maxlength attribute   120
Media

  print   31
  screen, handheld   28
Meta element <meta>   22
  author   22
  content attribute   22
  description   22
  expires   22
  generator   22
  http-equiv attribute   22
  keywords   22
  name attribute   22
  pragma, no-cache   24
  refresh   22
  revised   22
  robots, noindex   24
  scheme attribute   25
Method attribute   118
MIME types   98
Mobile Profile   178
Multipurpose Internet Mail Extension (MIME)   26

N

Name=value pair   118
Nested elements   18
No Frames element <noframes>   116
Noscript element <noscript>   26

O

Object element <object>   99
  classid attribute   104
  codebase attribute   106
  codetype attribute   102
  data attribute   99
  height attribute   99
  type attribute   99
  width attribute   99
Open Mobile Alliance (OMA)   11
Option element <option>   126
  multiple attribute   127
  selected attribute   127
  value attribute   126

Option group element <optgroup>   185
Ordered list element <ol>   60
   start attribute   179
   value attribute   179

P

Padding property
   padding shorthand rule   141
   padding-bottom rule   139
   padding-left rule   139
   padding-right rule   139
   padding-top rule   139
Page formats   174
Paragraph element <p>   17, 34
Parameter element <param>   103
   name attribute   103
   value attribute   103
Percentage % unit   73
PERL   118
Pixel abbreviation, px   73
Pixel px unit   69
Pointer   87
Post method, form submission   118
Preformat element <pre>   43
Print media   31
Profile attribute   20

Q

QuickTime media player   106
Quote element <q>   40

R

Radio buttons   124
Real media player   107
Rel attribute   28

Relative address   96
Relative em unit   140
Relative padding   140
Reset button   132
Rows attribute   112
Rowspan attribute   76

S

Sample element <samp>   45
Scheme attribute   25
Screen media   28, 148
Script element <script>   26
Scrolling attribute   114
Select element <select>   126
   name attribute   126
   size attribute   126
Selection menús   126
Selectors   50
Smaller text element <small>   183
Sound   104
Span element <span>   56
Spanning table columns   77
Spanning table rows   76
Square bullet   64
Src attribute   96, 111
Strong element <element>   42
Style attribute   181
Style element <style>   180
Stylesheet   28
Stylesheet clear rule   154
Stylesheet float rule   150
Stylesheet visibility rule   152
Submission form   118
Submit button   118
Summary attribute   72

T

Tab key   87
Tab order   92
Tabindex attribute   92
Table caption element <caption>   74

Table data element <td>   72
   abbr attribute   84
   align attribute   78
   colspan attribute   77
   headers attribute   81–82
   rowspan attribute   76
   valign attribute   79
Table element <table>   72
   summary attribute   72
Table heading element <th>   75
   abbr attribute   84
   align attribute   78
   axis attribute   82
   colspan attribute   77
   id attribute   81–82
   rowspan attribute   76
   scope attribute   80
   valign attribute   79
Table row element <tr>   72
   align attribute   78
   valign attribute   79
Target attribute   115
Target relationship   94
Text input box   120
Text-align property   161
Text-decoration property   162
Text-indent property   69, 163
Text-transform property   166
Textarea element <textarea>   128
   cols attribute   128
   name attribute   128
   rows attribute   128
Title element <title>   17, 21
   xml:lang attribute   21
Type attribute   26, 28, 98, 120

Unordered list element <ul>   61
URL address
   relative, absolute   27
Url term   168

Validation   12
Value attribute   120, 179
Variable element <var>   45
Video   105

Web page design   174
Width attribute   96
Wildcard ★   111–112
Wireless Markup Language (WML)   11
Word-spacing rule   164
WorldWide Web Consortium (W3C)   8
   Markup Validation Service   12
Wrapping text around images   150

XHTML Basic   11
XHTML Mobile Profile   178
XHTML root element   16
XML declaration   14
   encoding attribute   14
   version attribute   14